GREAT
BRITISH
SOUPS

120 tempting recipes from
Britain's master soup-makers

BOXTREE

First published 2016 by Boxtree
an imprint of Pan Macmillan
Pan Macmillan, 20 New Wharf Road, London N1 9RR
Associated companies throughout the world
www.panmacmillan.com

ISBN 978-0-7522-6571-1

Recipes by Glen Roberts
Copy-writing by Helen Amos and Lesley Loveday
Copy-editing by Anna Southgate
Art Direction, Styling and Design by Simon Daley at Giraffe Books
Recipe Photography by Ian Garlick
Food Styling by Valentina Harris, assisted by Ben Harris and Hannah Summers
Picture Research by Simon Daley at Giraffe Books

Printed in China

Contents

Introduction 6

Great British Favourites 26
Southwest England 50
Southeast England 68
The Midlands 82
Eastern England 98
Northwest England 122
Yorkshire and Northeast England 140
Wales 156
Northern Ireland 170
Scotland 186
Modern British 206
Multicultural Britain 232
On our Travels 272

Index 318

Introduction

In 1987, on a cold Saturday afternoon, a young man had been on a particularly treacherous sailing trip. He returned home to his parents' house, freezing and wet. It was the height of summer and his mum had made salad. Still cold, he asked if he could have some of her warming home-made soup… she hadn't made any. Why couldn't you buy quality, homely soup in the supermarkets? And then his idea was born…

The New Covent Garden Soup Co. started with a group of like-minded individuals whose first love was real, good food, and this philosophy remains at the heart of our business almost 30 years later. Since inception, we have created thousands of recipes and now we make enough soup each year to fill 28 Olympic-size swimming pools!

Created with the freshest produce in mind, soup still remains a favourite meal in many of our homes. Not only is soup highly versatile, but it's easy to make, packed full of nutritious ingredients and is a great way of using up leftovers. Health and nutrition are at the heart of all our recipes – whatever the occasion, we have a soup for you!

Our chefs lovingly create new recipes and frequently take inspiration from different areas of the UK. There is such diversity here – whether in the vegetables produced, the history of a region or in the many cultural influences that prevail. And it is this diversity that makes our very special 'Great Britain'.

Great British Soups is a collection of over 120 new soup recipes inspired by the different regions of Great Britain. Using ingredients that are synonymous with particular regions, a wide range of seasonal vegetables and the wisdom of our chefs, the recipes in this book have one common theme – Great Ingredients Speak for Themselves. And, of course, when you really have no time to cook at all, you will always find a carton or two of our wonderful soup on the shelf at your local store.

We hope you enjoy creating these delicious soups. Happy Souping.

THE NEW COVENT GARDEN SOUP TEAM

Tricks of the Trade

Although soup is, essentially, a very simple meal to cook, there are a few tricks of the trade that we thought you might like to know. The tips in this section of the book will make it even easier for you to produce a deliciously nutritious soup. We have done all the hard work for you, and all you need to do now is to get cooking!

Getting Started

The key to easy, fuss-free cooking is preparation. Always read a recipe in full before you start. Be confident that you have all the ingredients to hand and that you know what you are going to do.

'Mise en place', a common chef term, is translated as 'put in place'. It really pays to have all your preparation done up front: your ingredients peeled and trimmed, weighed and chopped. If you're not confident with multitasking, or you prefer your cooking experience to be a relaxed one, this will help you stay in control of a recipe and keep you stress-free.

When you are ready to start, put a damp cloth under your chopping board – this will stop it moving about as you work.

In all likelihood you are going to need a pan of water. It's so much quicker and more efficient to boil the kettle when you need hot water, rather than using a saucepan. And doing this saves hob space!

Cooking

Always use a big enough saucepan for making a soup. If in doubt, go one size bigger than your best guess. Ingredients cook better if they have space around them, and you don't want to worry about the soup spilling over the edges of the pan when you're blending!

When sweating onions, if they start to get too brown before they soften, add a splash of water. This will slow the cooking process down and the water will help the onions to soften. For a short while, the caramelisation process will stop. A few minutes later, the water will have evaporated and the onions will start to cook again.

If you want to make a creamy soup even creamier, but without adding calories, blend a handful of oats into the base. This will give the soup a thick, creamy finish (and oats are really good for you, too!).

Low and slow is the message for cooking a good soup. Unless a recipe states otherwise, take your time and simmer gently rather than boiling rapidly. Flavours develop much more fully when given time.

When you are adding herbs, it's usually advisable to add hard plants (thyme, rosemary, oregano) early on, so that they soften and develop flavour. Use soft herbs (parsley, chives, basil, dill) just before serving, to keep their freshness.

If a recipe uses cream or yoghurt, this should always be added just before the end of the cooking time, to avoid the soup splitting. When you do the final tasting, if your soup needs a little something extra, add a touch of lemon juice or vinegar. The acidity in these ingredients can really lift and enliven the flavour of your soup.

When you are sautéing ingredients in butter, add a little oil to the pan. It enables you to reach a higher temperature, and the butter is less likely to burn.

When roasting bones for stock, sprinkle a little milk powder over them before you put them in the oven. The milk powder causes a chemical reaction that enriches the meaty flavour. This is a very clever scientific trick called the 'maillard reaction'.

A recipe will always list an exact quantity of liquid to use – usually stock. However, it is generally a good idea not to add all of the liquid at once. Firstly, doing so enables you to adjust the thickness of your soup according to your liking. Secondly, other ingredients in a recipe will vary as to how they do or don't thicken the soup. For example, waxy potatoes may thicken a soup less than floury potatoes do. So hold a little back, in case you don't need it.

When you need to blend a soup, make sure the vegetables are really well cooked. Blend too early, and you risk the soup being grainy. There is one exception to this rule: potatoes, when really overcooked, can become starchy and glutinous.

Blending

When it comes to blending a soup, your main choices are a blender, a food processor or an immersion blender.

BLENDERS are great for puréeing soups. The only difficulty comes from the tricky process of transferring the hot soup to and from the blender itself. If you have time, allow the soup to cool a little beforehand. It is best to blend in batches and only to fill the blender halfway. Use the pulse a couple of times, ensuring that you are holding the lid down firmly (the steam will try to push the lid off). After a minute, take the lid off and let the steam escape. Now try blending, starting at a slightly slower speed and increasing it gradually.

FOOD PROCESSORS tend to chop a soup up into small pieces rather than puréeing it. This produces a soup with a slightly gritty texture and non-uniform pieces.

IMMERSION BLENDERS are the gadgets to use if you are striving for a perfect, creamy soup. You'll not have the mess of transferring the soup, because all the puréeing is done right in the saucepan. An immersion blender mashes even the tiniest particles into oblivion, delivering the smoothest, beautifully puréed soup. The trick to this, is to ensure that the head of the blender is fully immersed in the liquid before turning it on.

Ingredients

All ingredients lists state whether a fruit or vegetable is small, medium or large, and how to prepare it for cooking – finely or roughly chopped, cut into chunks, halved, quartered, and so on.

Unless otherwise stated, assume that all ingredients are prepared in the normal way: root vegetables, squashes and fruits are trimmed, peeled, cored, deseeded; leaves (kale, spinach, cavolo nero) are washed and destalked; dried legumes are rinsed; tinned vegetables are drained; peppers and chillies are deseeded; fish and shellfish are washed, descaled, peeled and deveined as applicable.

OILS It's not advisable to use expensive oils for sautéing, as heat changes the chemical structure and flavour of oils such as extra-virgin olive oil and sesame oil. Use rapeseed oil or a light olive oil instead.

ONIONS/SHALLOTS Onions are easier to peel if you keep the roots on when you cut them in half. There are many tips for peeling an onion without crying. Some suggest using a very sharp knife, others cutting the onions under water or freezing them for a few minutes before chopping. The reaction is linked to the fact that when an onion is cut, a small part of it produces an enzyme that reacts with the rest of the onion to release a gas. When that gas is mixed with water it creates an acid. And if this happens in your eyes it really stings!

GARLIC If you find peeling garlic fiddly, pop the separated cloves in a microwave for 10 seconds on full power. This will soften the skin and it will fall away from the flesh.

FRESH GINGER Peel ginger using a spoon. It is less wasteful than using a knife, and you won't cut yourself. If you freeze fresh ginger (already peeled), and grate it straight from the freezer you will avoid any stringy waste.

SPICES If possible, buy your spices in bulk from an Asian or Indian shop. This is much more economical than buying them in small jars or boxes from the supermarket. Toasting spices gives them a much more mellow flavour. Toast in larger quantities, if you like, and store them in airtight containers. Keep your spices out of direct sunlight to keep them fresher for longer.

HERBS When you chop herbs, freeze any excess in an ice-cube tray, so that you have ready-to-use portions for another time.

MEASUREMENTS All measurements for teaspoons and tablespoons are level, unless otherwise stated.

Your Pantry and Freezer

There are several ingredients that you should have in your pantry and freezer all year round. These are the oils, sauces, herbs and spices that really make a soup shine. There are some fibre providers in the list too – great for bulking out a soup for a more hearty treat. Once you've stocked up, these ingredients are just there, ready and waiting for you to cook.

IN YOUR PANTRY

Oils: for sautéing vegetables and finishing soups

Extra-virgin olive oil
Sunflower oil
Garlic oil
Basil oil
Chilli oil

Vinegars: great flavour enhancers

White wine vinegar
Red wine vinegar
Sherry vinegar
Balsamic vinegar

Beans and pulses: for adding fibre, protein and bulk

Lentils
Haricot beans
Cannellini beans
Chickpeas
Red kidney beans

Sauces and pastes: for instant added flavour

Mushroom ketchup
Worcestershire sauce
Horseradish sauce
Whole-grain mustard
Miso paste
Soy sauce
Mango chutney
Sun-dried tomato paste
Peanut butter
Honey
Maple syrup
Lemon juice
Lime juice

Quick cheats: for when you're pressed for time

Tinned chopped tomatoes
Passata
Stock cubes
Basil pesto
Thai curry paste
Grated Parmesan

Herbs and spices: soup essentials

Sea salt
Peppercorns
Ground cumin
Ground coriander
Turmeric
Garam masala
Chilli powder
Cayenne pepper
Smoked paprika
Saffron
Chilli flakes
Bay leaves
Dried thyme
Nutmeg

IN YOUR FREEZER

Frozen stocks
Chopped fresh herbs
Ginger
Chopped garlic
Pesto
Tapenade
Roast garlic purée
Butter

Stocks

A fresh, home-made stock turns a simple recipe into something really special: a meat stock adds richness and body in a way that a stock cube never can; a chicken stock adds a fresh silkiness that cannot be replicated; and a fish stock adds real depth of flavour.

Stock is the key to a great soup, yet many people are daunted by the prospect of making one. The secret is to leave the ingredients undisturbed. Resist the temptation to stir at any time, other than to skim impurities from the surface. Once you are familiar with the routine, stock-making can be therapeutic. It's also a great way to use your bones from a Sunday roast!

The stock recipes that follow make larger quantities than are needed for most recipes in this book. It is a great idea to make more than you need and freeze half of it for another time.

When choosing which stock to make, general advice is to match the main protein in your recipe – so a shellfish stock for a crab bisque; a beef stock for oxtail soup. If in doubt, use vegetable stock. Its lighter flavour will not mask that of the other ingredients.

Chicken Stock

A white, colourless stock involves simply simmering the bones to extract flavour. A brown or dark stock is one in which the bones and vegetables are roasted before being simmered, to give a richer flavour. Both use exactly the same ingredients.

MAKES 2 LITRES

1 raw chicken carcass or equivalent weight of chicken wings (or use a cooked chicken carcass from your Sunday roast)
2 medium onions, roughly chopped
2 medium carrots, roughly chopped
1 medium leek, roughly chopped
2 sticks celery, roughly chopped
1 bay leaf
10–12 black peppercorns
1 sprig thyme
2.2 litres water (or enough to cover)
Parsley stalks

WHITE STOCK Bring the ingredients to the boil in a large saucepan. Simmer gently for 3 hours. Every 20 minutes, skim any froth from the surface. Strain the stock through a fine sieve into a clean pan. Once settled, skim any fat from the top.

BROWN STOCK Roast the vegetables and chicken bones in a hot oven (200°C/gas mark 6) for 20 minutes to colour. Drain any fat from the tray, transfer the bones and vegetables to a large saucepan and continue the recipe as above.

Basic Brown Stock

This is similar to the dark chicken stock; using different types of meat adds subtlety to the flavours.

MAKES 3 LITRES

1.5kg raw beef, veal or lamb bones
4 medium onions, roughly chopped
5 medium carrots, roughly chopped
½ head celery, roughly chopped
2 bay leaves
10 black peppercorns
Few sprigs thyme
3.5 litres cold water (or enough to cover)

Place the bones and vegetables in a hot oven (200°C/gas mark 6) for 30 minutes to colour. Once roasted, transfer the bones and vegetables to a large saucepan. Take care not to add the fat from the bottom of the roasting tray. Add the remaining ingredients to the pan and cover with water.

Bring the stock to a simmer, and cook for 4 hours, skimming off any foam and impurities from the surface every 20 minutes or so. Strain through a fine sieve into a clean pan or bowl. When the stock has settled, skim any oil from the top. If you are using the stock later, allow to cool and lift off any set fat from the surface.

Ham Stock

A lesser-known stock than chicken or vegetable, this is bursting with the distinctive flavours of ham. The stock needs a good 4 hours to develop, but the end result is worth the wait. Most stocks offer an efficient way to use up bones from a meal that has already been eaten, but ham stock is at its best when the meat is cooked at the same time. You can then use the ham as an ingredient in many recipes.

MAKES 2 LITRES

1 medium ham hock
I large onion, roughly chopped
3 sticks celery, roughly chopped
3 large carrots, roughly chopped
4 cloves garlic, chopped
2 bay leaves
1 sprig rosemary or a few sage leaves (optional)
3–4 sprigs thyme
6 black peppercorns
2.2 litres water (or enough to cover)

Put all the ingredients in a large saucepan, cover with water by 5cm and bring to the boil. Skim the surface and reduce to a very low simmer. Skim any froth or grease from the surface every 20 minutes for the first hour. Simmer, uncovered, for 4 hours or until the ham is falling off the bone. Remove the ham hock and strain the stock through a fine sieve. Allow to cool, then cover and place in the fridge. Before you use the stock, remove any solidified fat from the surface.

Vegetable Stock

A stock should have enough flavour to be
easily identified, but not so much that it
overpowers other ingredients in a soup.
A vegetable stock makes a great basis for
many soups; without the more assertive
flavours found in the protein stocks it gives
other ingredients a chance to be the heroes.

MAKES 2 LITRES

3 large onions, roughly chopped
2 large carrots, roughly chopped
2 medium leeks, roughly chopped
½ head celery, roughly chopped
2 medium tomatoes, halved
1 bay leaf
4 sprigs parsley
2 sprigs thyme
5 black peppercorns
2 litres cold water

Heat all the ingredients in a large saucepan
and simmer for about 40 minutes. Strain
through a fine sieve.

Fish Stock

The distinct flavours of the fish make this
the perfect aromatic base for many soups.
It is much quicker to make than the meat
stocks, as it should only be left to simmer
for a very short time.

MAKE 2 LITRES

1.5kg white fish bones (cod, whiting, pollack, etc.)
4 sticks celery, roughly chopped
2 large carrots, roughly chopped
2 medium onions, roughly chopped
300ml white wine
1 bay leaf
4 sprigs parsley
10 black peppercorns
2.2 litres cold water

Put all the ingredients in a large saucepan.
Bring to the boil, uncovered, then lower the
heat and simmer for 20 minutes, but no
longer. Skim the froth from the surface
every few minutes, to remove any
impurities. Strain through a fine sieve.

Shellfish Stock

The flavour that comes from shellfish is quite astonishing. Simple to make, this is the perfect base for shellfish soups. Not only does it deliver a beautiful, concentrated flavour, but it ensures that you keep all of the goodness from the fish.

MAKES 2 LITRES

1kg shells from crab, lobster, prawns or a mix
1 medium onion, chopped
2 medium carrots, chopped
1 medium leek, chopped
3 sticks celery, chopped
125ml white wine or vermouth
2 tablespoons tomato purée
1 bay leaf
2.1 litres water
5 black peppercorns
5 cloves garlic
Parsley stalks

Lay the shells on a roasting tray and roast in a hot oven (200°C/gas mark 6) for 20 minutes. This gives a stronger flavour. Transfer the shells in a large saucepan with all the other ingredients. Cover with cold water and simmer for 40 minutes, skimming any froth from the surface occasionally. Strain through a fine sieve.

Basic Asian Broth

To make a really quick and healthy Asian broth base – one that you can add fresh vegetables and noodles to – simply take 1 litre of any other stock in the book and add these additional ingredients. This recipe is just a guideline; you can use endless combinations to suit your mood or taste. Add a touch of miso paste, a shake of Chinese five-spice powder, or a splash of sesame oil or fish sauce.

MAKES 1.2 LITRES

4 thin slices fresh root ginger
3–4 slices red chilli
Soy sauce, to taste
Rice wine or Shaoxing vinegar, to taste
1 stick lemongrass, bruised
200ml coconut milk
I clove garlic, sliced
1 litre stock
½ lime, juiced

Place all the ingredients except the lime juice in a large saucepan and pour in the stock. Simmer for 10 minutes, to release the flavours. Add the lime juice, then strain through a fine sieve.

Garnishes and Accompaniments

A garnish can look fabulous and adds an extra element of taste. Use it to introduce a contrasting colour, flavour or texture, or to bring a minor ingredient to the forefront. Garnishes can also be exquisite visually: a dollop of yoghurt looks stunning in a rich dark-green pea soup. Here are a selection of recipes that will help you find inspiration for serving the soups in this book.

Fresh Herbs
Chives, basil, dill, lovage and parsley are all lovely sprinkled on top of a soup. Have fun experimenting with the different textures and flavours that they can add.

Celery Flowers
When you use celery in your recipe, keep the lovely fragrant inner leaves to garnish your soup with at the end.

Flavoured Oils
A drizzle of oil looks beautiful swirled into the top of your soup and can add a great extra flavour. To make your own, use a good-quality olive oil and add your flavouring. Leave to infuse for as long as possible, but for at least a good couple of hours. You can add pretty much anything that takes your fancy – dried chilli flakes, fresh herbs and pumpkin seeds are a good starting point.

Flavoured Butters
To make a luxurious and indulgent topping for your soup, soften some butter in a bowl and mix in whatever takes your fancy. Place on a sheet of cling film or baking parchment and roll into a long sausage shape. Place in the fridge – it will keep for about a week. When you are ready to use, simply take a little slice and add to the top of your bowl of soup.

BASIC HERB BUTTER RECIPE To 250g softened butter add 1 teaspoon chopped chives, 1 teaspoon chopped parsley, the zest of 1 lemon and 1 pinch sea salt.

OTHER THINGS YOU COULD ADD Dried or fresh chilli, lemon zest, poppy seeds, toasted crushed spices.

Dairy Toppings
A dollop of something dairy adds an unbeatable creaminess to a soup. Any of the following work, added at the end so the soup doesn't split: sour cream; crème fraiche; yoghurt; crumbled goat's cheese.

Toasted Halloumi Squares
Cut a block of halloumi into squares, drizzle with olive oil and flash under the grill until golden. Drop into your soup as an alternative to croutons.

Cheddar Chilli Crisps

Grate 200g Cheddar into a bowl and add 1 pinch chilli flakes. Divide into 10 mounds on a non-stick-paper-lined baking tray. Pat each mound flat, leaving a space between each and pop in a preheated oven (160°C/ gas mark 4) for 20 minutes, until golden and crispy. Allow to cool for 5 minutes, then pat dry on kitchen paper and serve.

Rarebit Croutons

Dating back to the 18th century, Welsh rarebit is a scrumptious version of cheese on toast. Add this to the top of our Welsh Leek and Caerphilly Cheese (see page 167).

Preheat the grill. Melt 50g butter in a saucepan over a low heat and add 120ml milk. Stir in 40g grated Cheddar, until melted. Add 1 teaspoon mustard powder and 1 tablespoon Worcestershire sauce. Season with salt and 1 pinch cayenne pepper. Toast 3 slices thick bread on both sides, then spread with the rarebit mix. Return to the grill and cook until browned. Allow to cool and chop into squares.

Cheesy Croutes

This classic accompaniment to French onion soup works beautifully with our Newcastle Brown Onion soup (see page 147).

Preheat the grill. Cut a French stick into finger-thick slices. Rub with 1 clove garlic and lightly brush with oil. Toast under the grill on both sides, sprinkle generously with grated Gruyère cheese and return to the grill until melting and lovely.

For a bowl of minestrone (see page 237), brush the toasted croutes with oil on one side and top with a little pesto and some shavings of Parmesan cheese, then melt.

For a cauliflower or celeriac soup, top your toasted croutes with crumbled Stilton or Shropshire Blue and gently melt.

For a tomato soup, try brushing the toasts with a little cranberry sauce and crumbled goat's cheese before grilling.

Crispy Wedges

Cut 3 large potatoes lengthwise, to make 25–30 wedges. Place in a saucepan and cover with stock (any meat stock is fine). Add a few sprigs thyme, 1 bay leaf and pepper. Parboil until the wedges are just starting to soften, about 15 minutes. Drain carefully, then return to the pan. Add salt, 2 tablespoons oil, 1 knob butter and toss gently. Line a baking tray with non-stick paper and lay the wedges in rows. Tip the rest of the butter and oil over the wedges and bake in a hot oven (200°C/gas mark 6) for 20 minutes, until crispy and golden. Reheat when ready to serve. Perfect with our Lancashire Hotpot (see page 133).

Crispy Pancetta

Lay slices of pancetta between two sheets of non-stick paper and place between two baking trays. Bake in a hot oven (200°C/gas mark 6) for 10 minutes, until crispy and flat. Pat dry on kitchen paper. This is great crumbled into pea-based soups.

Pancetta-wrapped Breadsticks

Cut a stale French stick into lengths measuring 10 x 2cm. Drizzle with olive oil and spiral a slice of raw pancetta around each one. Lay on a non-stick baking tray and bake in a hot oven (200°C/gas mark 6) until crispy. Sprinkle with grated Parmesan and serve alongside your soup.

Bacon and Maple Popcorn

Heat a dry frying pan and fry two rashers of bacon until crispy, then finish cooking in a hot oven (200°C/gas mark 6) until really dry. Allow to cool and chop finely. Heat 2 tablespoons maple syrup in the bacon pan. As it starts to bubble, add the chopped bacon and 1 handful plain popcorn. A great alternative to croutons.

Crispy Pasta Bows

Dust some cooked and well-drained pasta bows with paprika and onion powder. Deep-fry until crisp and golden. Drain on kitchen paper and pop on top of your soup.

Seeded Pitta Chips

Slice some pitta bread into about ten triangles and roll in a little oil. Add some salt and poppy seeds and lay on a baking tray. Bake at 180°C/gas mark 4 until crisp.

Smoky Pepitas

Roll a handful of pumpkin seeds in a little vegetable oil. Add 1 pinch paprika, cayenne, cumin and sea salt. Lay on a non-stick baking tray and bake at 180°C/gas mark 4 for 5 minutes. Allow to cool, and sprinkle on your spicy soups. Store in a mason jar.

Pesto

You cannot beat home-made pesto. Spread 1 good handful pine nuts out over a roasting tray and roast in a hot oven (180°C/gas mark 4) for 10 minutes, or until golden brown. Add to the bowl of a food processor, along with 1 good handful grated Parmesan and 3 good handfuls basil. With the food processor on, drizzle 2 tablespoons olive oil into the bowl until you reach the desired consistency. Season and add more olive oil if needed. Swirl into a soup before serving.

Pico de Gallo Salsa

The name of this fresh salsa translates as 'rooster's beak'. It originated in Mexico and is great with any soup, but especially our Vegetarian Feijoada (see page 314).
Mix together 1 finely diced medium onion, 1 deseeded and finely chopped ripe tomato, and 1–2 deseeded and finely chopped jalapeño chillies. Add a good handful chopped coriander and the juice of 1 lime. Sprinkle with salt and ½ teaspoon crushed, toasted cumin seeds. Stir and leave to marinate for 10 minutes. Adjust the chilli, lime and salt to suit your taste.

Breads

Imagine a steaming bowl of soup, and thoughts of a crusty roll or a hunk of bread generously spread with butter are not far behind. Whether you're dipping the bread in as you eat, to soak up the soup's flavours, or using it to mop up the last tasty drops from the bowl, there is no doubt that the two make a perfect combination.

Like soup, bread is a traditional food that features in many cultures. From Italian focaccia to Irish soda bread and Indian flatbreads, it has been a staple throughout history. Prepared from a dough of flour and water, it is thought to be one of the oldest foods created by humans.

With so many different breads to choose from, we have selected just a few of our favourites. Experiment with these, and other recipes, to find perfect bread/soup combination. It's such a great way to start baking and nothing beats the smell of 'fresh from the oven' home-baked bread.

Boxty

This traditional Irish potato pancake is simple to make and provides a great accompaniment for our Colcannon with Ham Hock (see page 183).

MAKES 12

500g raw potatoes, grated and squeezed of all liquid
500g leftover mashed potato
450g flour
4g baking powder
3 spring onions, chopped
400ml buttermilk
1 egg
2 tablespoons oil
Pinch salt
Pinch pepper

Place the grated and mashed potatoes in a bowl. Sift in the flour and the baking powder. Add the chopped spring onions.

Combine the buttermilk with the egg, and incorporate this into the potato mix, a little at a time. You may not need all the liquid – the mixture should be like a heavy batter.

Heat the oil in a heavy frying pan. When the oil is just starting to smoke, use a tablespoon to drop spoonfuls of the boxty mixture into the pan. They will spread out a little. Cook for 4 minutes on each side; the boxty should be golden brown, with the raw potato soft and cooked.

Focaccia

This oven-baked Italian bread is similar in style and texture to pizza dough. You can top it with all sorts of different ingredients.

MAKES 1 LOAF

7g sachet dried yeast
380ml tepid water
500g strong white flour, plus extra for dusting
1½ teaspoons salt
2 tablespoons olive oil, plus extra for brushing
Good pinch flaked sea salt
Handful rosemary sprigs

Preheat the oven to 180°C/gas mark 4. Whisk the dried yeast into the tepid water and allow to rest for 10 minutes.

Tip the flour and salt into a large bowl, then add the water and yeast mixture and the oil. Mix together. Tip the dough out onto a lightly floured worktop and knead it for a good 10 minutes. Brush with a little more oil, return to the bowl, and cover for about 1 hour, or until it doubles in size.

Brush a large baking tray with olive oil and place the dough on it. Using your fingers, stretch the dough to make a 25 x 25cm square. Cover, and allow to rise again for 40 minutes.

When the dough has risen by half its height, use your fingers to make holes in the bread. Brush with more olive oil and sprinkle with salt and rosemary. Bake in the preheated oven for 35 minutes.

Flatbread

Rolled incredibly flat before baking, this unleavened dough is thought to be the earliest form of bread. It makes a fantastic accompaniment to some of our spicy soups. For a different flavour, add some chopped chives and coriander to the dough before rolling. Alternatively, pat a mixture of crushed spices (cumin seeds, coriander seeds) into the flatbreads after rolling.

MAKES 10

300g self-raising flour, plus extra for dusting
200ml water
1 tablespoon olive oil
1 teaspoon salt

Mix the ingredients together in a large bowl. When the dough comes away cleanly from the sides of the bowl, transfer it to a lightly floured work surface and knead for a few minutes, Cover with the empty bowl and rest for 20 minutes.

Sprinkle more flour on to your work surface and divide the dough into ten balls. Roll each ball into a disc measuring about 2mm in thickness.

Heat a heavy frying pan or griddle plate. Make sure it's hot to start with, then adjust the heat as you work – you'll soon get the hang of how hot the pan needs to be. Cook the flatbreads, one or two at a time, for a few minutes on each side. Keep them warm on a plate covered with a clean cloth.

Stottie Cakes

Stottie is unleavened bread from the North of England. It goes well with our Pease Pudding and Saveloy recipe (see page 144).

MAKES 6

280g butter, plus extra for greasing
1550g strong white flour, plus extra for dusting
6 teaspoons salt
Pinch white pepper
3 teaspoons dried yeast
3 teaspoons sugar
450ml warm water
450ml warm milk

Preheat the oven to 200°C/gas mark 6. In a bowl, rub the butter into the flour, salt and pepper, until it resembles breadcrumbs.

In a jug, mix the yeast and sugar with 150ml warm water, and wait for it to froth. Make a well in the centre of the flour, then gradually add all the remaining liquids and combine to make a dough. Knead for a few minutes, until smooth and elastic, then place in a lightly oiled large bowl, covered with oiled cling film. Leave somewhere warm to double in size. This will take at least 1 hour.

Place the dough on a floured board. Divide into six and flatten each into a large disc, about 2cm thick. Prick the top of each disc with a fork, place on a greased baking tray and leave in a warm place for 20 minutes, to rise again.

Bake for 15 minutes, then quickly turn the bread over and bake for a further 5 minutes.

Seeded Soda Bread

This Irish loaf is really easy to make. We've added seeds to our recipe, but you can add anything you like to create different flavours. Try butter, raisins, cheese or nuts.

MAKES 1 LOAF

200g white flour, plus extra for dusting
200g wholemeal flour
50g pinhead oats
10g mixed seeds (millet, quinoa, sunflower)
1 teaspoon salt
1 teaspoon bicarbonate of soda
1 tablespoon honey
400ml buttermilk

Preheat the oven to 180°C/gas mark 4 and line a baking tray with non-stick paper.

Tip all the dry ingredients into a large mixing bowl and make a well in the centre.

Combine the honey and buttermilk, then tip into the well. Using a round-bladed dinner knife, mix the ingredients together (this stops your hands from getting caked up and helps prevent overworking the dough). Once most of the liquid has been absorbed, dust your hands lightly with flour and finish mixing the dough by hand. Do not overwork. The dough isn't like a normal bread dough – it isn't smooth – so don't worry too much about texture.

Place the dough on the lined baking tray and shape into a rough circle. Use a knife to make a cross in the top and bake for about 50 minutes.

Great British Favourites

It has been wonderful exploring the culinary highlights of our great land to write the recipes for this book. On a cold winter's day, soup lifts our spirits and comforts our soul; it keeps us warm and soothes us when we're ill. Traditionally making use of leftover food, soup is intrinsic to our island cuisine and owes as much to a British sense of thrift as it does to our blustery climate.

With so many beautiful ingredients and historic traditions specific to different areas of Britain, it has been hard to make our final selection. As always, however, there were a number of recipes that we simply couldn't ignore on account of their heritage alone. These are the recipes that represent the very heart of our nation's soup-making history. They evoke memories of crisp, chilly days and joyful family meals. Think Leek and Potato, Brown Windsor and London Particular … without them a book on soups would be incomplete. These are some of our finest soup recipes, and we hope you enjoy making them.

Leek and Potato

One of our all-time favourites, this soup recipe should be in everyone's repertoire. Creamy and warming, this filling one-pot meal is simply delicious with a chunk of warm bread. Sprinkle with a garnish of spring onions and parsley for a home-cooked delight.

Melt the butter in a large saucepan and add the onion. Sweat until the onion loses colour, about 10 minutes, then add the leeks and cook for a further 5 minutes, until soft. Cover the pan between stirs.

Add the potatoes and the stock to the pan, cover, and simmer for 20 minutes, or until the potatoes begin to break apart.

Add the milk, cream, lemon juice and seasoning, and blend the soup until you reach your preferred texture – we think smooth is best.

Reheat the soup and garnish with the spring onions and parsley before serving.

6 SERVINGS

20 MINUTES PREPARATION

40 MINUTES COOKING

40g butter
1 large onion, finely sliced
4 large leeks, finely sliced
600g floury potatoes, cut into chunks
1 litre vegetable stock
100ml milk
130ml single cream
½ lemon, juiced
Salt
White pepper
6 spring onions, finely chopped
Good handful parsley, finely chopped

Brown Windsor

A Victorian favourite, Brown Windsor was once a staple in restaurants and, of course, at Windsor Castle. But this hearty soup suffered during the Second World War, when the ravages of wartime economy meant the only characteristic it shared with pre-war versions was its brownness! Based on an early-20th century recipe, our soup returns this British classic to its former glory. It's time to put Brown Windsor back on the menu.

Heat the oil and the butter in a large pan and, without overcrowding, brown off the meat. Do this in stages if need be, then remove the meat from the pan and reserve.

Add the vegetables to the pan and stir, adding a little more oil if needed. Sweat over a low heat for 10 minutes, then add the flour and cook for a little longer.

Return the browned meat to the pan and add the pearl barley, stock, Worcestershire sauce, herbs and seasoning. Bring to the boil and simmer gently for about an hour, or until the meat is tender and falling apart. Remove the bay leaf, check the seasoning and serve with crusty bread.

6 SERVINGS

15 MINUTES PREPARATION

1½ HOURS COOKING

2 tablespoons oil

50g butter

250g trimmed stewing beef, cut into 2cm chunks

250g trimmed lamb neck fillet, cut into 2cm chunks

1 large onion, wedged

2 medium carrots, cut into chunks

2 sticks celery, cut into half-moon slices

1 heaped tablespoon flour

100g dried pearl barley

1.5 litres beef stock

1 tablespoon Worcestershire sauce

1 bay leaf

1 sprig rosemary, needles removed and chopped

Good pinch black pepper

Good pinch salt

Lentil and Bacon

Our traditional Lentil and Bacon soup is a firm favourite – a mouth-watering recipe packed with lentils that will keep you fuller for longer. This is a complex soup, with many layers of flavour, from the smokiness of the bacon, through the earthiness of the lentils, to the mild sweetness of the onions and carrots and the acidity of the tomatoes. Delicious.

Heat the oil in a large saucepan and fry the bacon to give it some colour. Add the vegetables and cook for 15 minutes to give them colour, then add the garlic.

Add the spices to the pan and cook for 1–2 minutes, stirring, then add the herbs and the tomato purée and cook for a few minutes more.

Add the lentils, pearl barley and stock and simmer for 40–60 minutes, until the lentils are soft. Finally, add the kale and simmer for 10 minutes.

Discard the bay leaf, then remove a few ladlefuls of the soup and blend for just a few seconds before returning to the pan. This will bring it all together perfectly.

6 SERVINGS

10 MINUTES PREPARATION

1 HOUR COOKING

2 tablespoons oil
180g smoked bacon lardons, chopped
1 large onion, finely chopped
2 sticks celery, chopped
3 medium carrots, diced
3 cloves garlic, crushed
1 teaspoon smoked paprika
Good pinch ground cumin
2 sprigs thyme
1 bay leaf
2 sage leaves, chopped
2 tablespoons tomato purée
65g red lentils
75g puy lentils
40g dried pearl barley
1.3 litres ham or chicken stock
30g kale, chopped

Bubble and Squeak

An old English tradition, bubble and squeak is typically made using shallow-fried leftover vegetables from a roast dinner. The main ingredients are potato and cabbage but carrots, peas, Brussels sprouts or any other leftover vegetables can be added too. The charming name of this dish is thought to derive from the bubbling and squeaking that emerged from the pan in the days of cooking over an open fire.

Heat half the oil in a large saucepan and sauté the onions for 10 minutes – you want them to be soft and a little browned at the edges. Remove from the pan and reserve.

Heat the remaining oil in the same pan and fry off the meat. Allow it to get quite crispy then remove and reserve.

Still using the same pan, heat the chicken stock and milk, add the cooked potatoes and warm for 5 minutes. Break the potatoes down a little using a potato masher, leaving a few chunks. Add the cooked vegetables, the cooked cabbage, the spring onions and the browned meat and onions. Add more stock, depending on how thick you want the soup to be.

Bring to a simmer and season. Ladle the soup into bowls and top with a little butter if you're feeling indulgent!

6 SERVINGS

10 MINUTES PREPARATION

30 MINUTES COOKING

2 tablespoons olive oil

2 large onions, sliced

400g cold cuts – anything you have: roast chicken, boiled ham, sausages, cooked bacon or a mixture, chopped

700ml chicken stock

130ml milk

650g leftover cooked potatoes or mash

120g leftover cooked vegetables: peas, carrots, green beans, all roughly chopped

100g cooked cabbage, chopped

4 spring onions, finely chopped

Salt

Black pepper

Knob cold butter (optional, for serving)

Glen's London Particular

This soup takes its name from the dense 'peasouper' fogs that often descended upon London during the industrial age. Glen Roberts, our soup development chef, has added his twist by using ham hock rather than bacon for a more luxuriant depth of flavour. This soup should be kept thick and hearty, and is best served with warm crusty bread.

Melt the butter in a large saucepan and sweat the vegetables for 5 minutes. Add the split peas.

Pour in the stock and bring to a simmer. Put a lid on the pan and cook gently for 30 minutes, or until the peas are really soft. Remove from the heat, remove a little of the soup, blend it and return to the pan.

Add the pulled ham, parsley and seasoning to finish.

6 SERVINGS

10 MINUTES PREPARATION

40 MINUTES COOKING

50g butter
1 large onion, chopped
2 sticks celery, chopped
1 large carrot, chopped
220g dried green split peas, soaked overnight then rinsed and drained
1.7 litres ham stock
250g pulled ham hock
10g parsley, chopped
Salt
Coarse black pepper

Mulligatawny

The name 'mulligatawny' comes from two Tamil words *milaku*, meaning 'pepper' and *tanni*, meaning 'water'. The ingredient that gives the soup such a delicious, rich flavour is curry powder. Give this soup a really authentic touch by serving it with warm naan bread, a dollop of yoghurt and a sprinkle of fragrant coriander.

Heat the oil in a large saucepan and sauté the onion and peppers for 10 minutes. Add the garlic, ginger, chilli and spices and cook for 1 minute longer.

Add the tomato purée and apple, followed by the rice and lentils. Coat the rice and lentils with the other ingredients, then add the chopped tomatoes, tamarind paste and stock.

Simmer for 20 minutes. Ensure the rice and lentils are nearly cooked before adding the chicken and simmer for a further 5 minutes.

Finally, stir in the spring onions and season to taste. Garnish with a dollop of yoghurt and coriander, if desired.

6 SERVINGS

15 MINUTES PREPARATION

40 MINUTES COOKING

2 tablespoons ghee or oil

1 medium onion, sliced

2 medium red peppers, diced

5 cloves garlic, crushed

Thumb-sized piece root ginger, grated

Pinch chilli powder

1 teaspoon ground coriander

1 teaspoon ground cumin

1 teaspoon mild curry powder

50g tomato purée

1 medium apple, grated

80g long-grain rice

25g dried red lentils

500g tinned chopped tomatoes

1 teaspoon tamarind paste

1 litre chicken stock

200g cooked chicken, shredded

3 spring onions, finely sliced

Salt

Black pepper

60ml natural yoghurt
(optional, for serving)

Good handful coriander, chopped
(optional, for serving)

Smoked Haddock Kedgeree

Kedgeree is a traditional Anglo-Indian dish of rice and smoked fish. The word 'kedgeree' derives from the Hindi word *khichri*, meaning 'edible mashup'. Our soupy version balances the spicy and smoky flavours of its ingredients and makes the perfect choice for lunch or a light supper.

Place the fish in a large saucepan with the milk and add the bay leaf. Bring to the boil and remove from the heat. Allow to cool, then remove the fish from the milk, discard any skin and bones and flake the flesh. Put the fish to one side, then strain and reserve the cooking liquid for later.

Melt the butter in a large saucepan and sweat the onion for 10 minutes. Add the spices to the pan and cook for a few minutes longer.

Add the cauliflower, the stock and the reserved milk. Simmer gently for 20 minutes. Once all the vegetables are soft, blend the soup.

Add the rice to the pan and cook for 20 minutes, or until the rice has cooked.

Add the flaked fish to the soup with half the spring onions and parsley, and the yoghurt. Season, and ladle the soup into bowls. Top with boiled egg halves and the remaining spring onions and parsley.

6 SERVINGS

20 MINUTES PREPARATION

1 HOUR COOKING

400g uncoloured smoked haddock
280ml milk
1 bay leaf
60g butter
1 large onion, finely diced
2 teaspoons mild curry powder
1 teaspoon paprika
Pinch cayenne pepper
1 small cauliflower, roughly chopped
1.5 litres fish or vegetable stock
150g long-grain rice
3 spring onions, chopped
10g parsley, chopped
40ml natural yoghurt or
single cream
Salt
Black pepper
3 soft-boiled eggs, peeled and
halved, to serve

Chicken and Root Vegetable

You can't beat a big bowl of chicken soup, and this hearty version certainly won't disappoint. We have taken succulent chicken and classic root vegetables — carrot, celeriac and swede — and married them with pearl barley, parsley and thyme. For a richer, more intense flavour, use one of our Chicken Stock recipes (see page 12).

Melt the butter in a large saucepan and sweat the onion, half the carrots, the celery and the garlic for 10 minutes.

Add the stock to the pan and simmer for 30 minutes, then blend until smooth.

Add the pearl barley, celeriac, swede, remaining carrots and the herbs, and cook for 40 minutes, until the barley and the vegetables are cooked. Remove the bay and the thyme.

Add the cooked chicken, parsley and seasoning, and serve.

6 SERVINGS

20 MINUTES PREPARATION

1 HOUR 20 MINUTES COOKING

50g butter
1 large onion, finely diced
4 large carrots, finely diced
3 sticks celery, diced
3 cloves garlic, crushed
1 litre chicken stock
30g dried pearl barley
½ medium celeriac, chopped
½ medium swede, chopped
1 bay leaf
2 sprigs thyme
200g cooked chicken, shredded
Good handful parsley, chopped
Salt
Coarse black pepper

Chicken Noodle

Comforting and full of love, this is the soup we all remember most from our childhood. To enrich the flavour, use one of our Chicken Stock recipes (see page 12). Go on, take a step back in time and turn to our easy and delicious Chicken Noodle Soup when you're feeling under the weather.

Heat the oil in a large saucepan and gently sauté the vegetables for 10 minutes.

Add the chicken stock to the pan and simmer for 15 minutes, or until the vegetables are almost cooked.

Add the pasta and the chicken to the soup and simmer for 10 minutes, or until the pasta is cooked.

Finally, add the parsley, season and serve.

6 SERVINGS

10 MINUTES PREPARATION

40 MINUTES COOKING

2 tablespoons oil
2 medium carrots, diced
2 sticks celery, sliced
1 large onion, chopped
1.5 litres chicken stock
60g spaghetti or noodles, broken into short lengths
320g cooked chicken, chopped or shredded
Good pinch chopped parsley
Salt
Black pepper

Festive Supper

From the turkey to the sprouts, the mince pies to the party puddings, whatever festive feast you're throwing this Christmas, you'll love our Festive Supper. With all the classic ingredients from your Christmas meal, this really is Christmas in a bowl!

Heat the oil in a large saucepan and fry the bacon until light golden in colour. Throw in the sage leaves and fry for a little longer. Remove from the pan and set aside.

Using the same pan, add the onion, celery and garlic and soften for 10 minutes. Add the cauliflower, potato and herbs and cook for a few minutes longer.

Pour in the stock, add the nutmeg, if using, and cook for 20 minutes. Remove the bay leaf and blend the soup.

Add the remaining ingredients to the soup, along with the cooked bacon, and warm through before serving. If you prefer, hold back the cranberries and chestnuts and use them to garnish the soup.

6 SERVINGS

15 MINUTES PREPARATION

50 MINUTES COOKING

10ml oil

200g bacon or pancetta, cubed

5 sage leaves, chopped

1 large onion, chopped

2 sticks celery, chopped

1 clove garlic, chopped

1 medium cauliflower, chopped

1 medium potato, chopped

2 sprigs thyme

1 bay leaf

1.2 litres chicken or ham stock

Pinch ground nutmeg (optional)

200g cooked turkey meat, shredded

150g cooked chipolatas or sausages, sliced

150g cooked sprouts or cabbage, roughly chopped

20g dried cranberries, chopped

25ml single cream

20g cooked chestnuts, roughly chopped

Salt

Pinch coarse black pepper

Southwest
England

Lush countryside, dramatic rural landscapes, quaint fishing villages and pretty coastal scenery combine to make the South West. This is one of the country's largest regions, comprising the counties of Gloucestershire, Wiltshire, Somerset, Dorset, Devon and Cornwall, as well as the Isles of Scilly. It may surprise you to learn that the northern edge of Gloucestershire is as close to the Scottish border as it is to the southwestern tip of Cornwall.

This region has a plethora of indigenous gourmet delights from clotted cream to the infamous Cornish pasty, a traditional favourite of West Country miners who carried these beef and vegetable pies in their pockets to warm their hands and bellies. The county of Somerset has always had a strong association with apples, and supports tiny orchards making scrumpy as well as large operations selling apple brandy. With such an extensive coastline it's no surprise that many of the recipes from this region favour ingredients from the sea. It is said that the superb quality of the shellfish is linked to the cleanliness of the water; crystal clear and nutrient-rich. Salcombe crabs are sweet, delicately flavoured and packed with vitamins. They provide the perfect base for our crab soup recipe, while scallops are the centrepiece for our smooth pea and chorizo creation.

Cornish Red Mullet and Monkfish

The Cornish coastline has one of Britain's best suppliers of red mullet and monkfish. Here, they combine with an aromatic blend of vegetables and the distinct taste of anchovies. Great served with crusty bread and a dollop of garlic mayonnaise, this soup will have you reaching for a second bowl.

Heat the oil in a large saucepan and gently sauté the onion, carrot, celery and fennel for 10 minutes. Add the garlic and anchovies and cook for a further 10 minutes.

Add the orange zest, saffron, white wine and bay to the pan. Season and cook for 1 minute. Pour in the stock and add the tinned tomatoes. Cover the pan and simmer for 30 minutes.

Remove the bay leaf and orange zest then blend the soup. Add the potatoes and cook for 20 minutes, until the potatoes are soft.

Drop the cut monkfish into the simmering soup and cook for 5 minutes, before adding the red mullet, lemon juice and parsley. Stir gently.

Put the lid on the pan and remove from the heat. Leave to stand for 5 minutes – the heat should be enough to finish cooking the fish.

6 SERVINGS

20 MINUTES PREPARATION

1 HOUR 20 MINUTES COOKING

2 tablespoons olive oil
1 large onion, finely sliced
1 medium carrot, chopped
4 sticks celery, finely sliced
1 medium fennel, finely sliced
3 cloves garlic, crushed
3–4 tinned anchovies
1 piece orange zest
Good pinch saffron
150ml white wine
1 bay leaf
900ml fish stock
400g tinned chopped tomatoes
220g Charlotte potatoes, quartered
215g monkfish fillets,
cut into chunks
215g red mullet fillets,
cut into chunks
½ lemon, juiced
Good handful flat-leaf
parsley, chopped
Salt
Black pepper

Nikki's Cornish Fish Chowder

This scrumptious fish chowder is the creation of our communications guru, Nikki Churchill. Thick, creamy and rustic, it's a hearty soup with deep flavours and a luxurious texture. Adding bacon brings a welcome smokiness. Once you have made this chowder a few times, you will begin to understand the Zen of chowder and why Nikki was so eager to spread the word!

Lay the haddock in a large frying pan, add the milk and the bay leaf and bring to the boil. Cook for 5 minutes (or longer for a thick fillet). Remove the fish from the pan and flake into chunks, discarding any skin and bones.

While the fish is cooking, melt the butter in a large saucepan and sweat the onion, leeks and bacon for 5 minutes. Do not allow to brown.

Add the diced potatoes to the pan with the stock. Season, bearing in mind that the haddock may already be quite salty. Put a lid on the pan and bring to the boil. Lower the heat and simmer for 10–15 minutes, until the potatoes are tender.

Add the prawns and the squid rings to the pan and simmer for a further 5 minutes.

Strain the fish milk into the soup, discarding the bay leaf, and add the haddock chunks and sweetcorn. Simmer for 1–2 minutes.

Scatter with the parsley and serve in big bowls with warm crusty bread with butter.

4 SERVINGS

20 MINUTES PREPARATION

35 MINUTES COOKING

450g uncoloured smoked haddock
450ml milk
1 bay leaf
25g butter
1 medium onion, chopped
2 medium leeks, sliced
4 rashers smoked streaky bacon, diced
450g floury potatoes, diced
450ml fish or vegetable stock
12 king prawns, halved if very large
2 small squid tubes, cut into rings
195g tinned sweetcorn, drained
2 tablespoons roughly chopped parsley
Salt
Pepper

Laura's Pea, Chorizo and Scallop

This soup was developed by our marketing expert Laura McIntosh. The combination of chorizo and scallops makes a classic centrepiece for the silky, smooth pea soup. Both vibrant and delicious, it reminds Laura of holidays on the south coast.

Heat the olive oil in a large saucepan and sauté the shallots and garlic until soft.

Add the chicken stock to the pan and bring to the boil. Add the petit pois and simmer for 3–4 minutes, adding the spinach for the last minute.

Blend the soup and pass through a fine sieve. Stir in the butter and warm through.

Dry-fry the chorizo for 3–4 minutes, until brown. Remove the chorizo and cook the scallops in the same oil for 2–4 minutes, turning halfway through.

Pour the soup into bowls and top with the chorizo and scallops before serving.

6 SERVINGS

10 MINUTES PREPARATION

15 MINUTES COOKING

2 tablespoons olive oil
8 small shallots, chopped
2 cloves garlic, chopped
800ml chicken stock
1kg petit pois
2 small handfuls spinach
1 large knob butter
150g chorizo, diced
24 small or 12 large scallops

Somerset White Onion and Cider

There's something so incredibly humble about onion soup. Easy to make, this soup is delicious. It allows onion fans to get that sharp, pungent hit, but within gentle, velvety surroundings. And with a warming dash of cider to boot!

Melt the butter in a large saucepan and gently sweat the onions, bay and sage until the onions become transluscent. This will take a good 30 minutes. Keep a lid on between stirs, and add a little of the cider or stock if need be, to prevent the onions browning.

Pour in the cider and stock and cook for a further 20 minutes.

Stir in the cream and season. Remove the herbs and blend the soup before serving.

6 SERVINGS

15 MINUTES PREPARATION

1 HOUR COOKING

100g butter
6 large onions, sliced
1 bay leaf
1 sage leaf
200ml cider or white wine
800ml vegetable stock
40ml double cream
Salt
Pepper

Pulled Somerset Ham, Celeriac and Parsley

Smooth, warming and delicious, this simple soup combines the great taste of pulled ham with the distinctive tang of apples that is only found in Somerset cider. You won't be able to resist it.

Melt the butter in a large saucepan and sweat the onion for 10 minutes, until colourless. Add the celeriac and sweat for a further 5 minutes.

Stir in the cider and the stock, put a lid on the pan, and simmer for 30 minutes, until the celeriac is soft.

Add the crème fraiche to the soup and blend.

Finally, add the pulled ham hock and parsley to the soup, reheat and serve.

6 SERVINGS

15 MINUTES PREPARATION

40 MINUTES COOKING

50g butter

1 medium onion, finely chopped

1 large celeriac, roughly chopped

150ml cider

1.2 litres ham or chicken stock

70g crème fraiche

300g pulled ham hock

Good handful parsley, chopped

Somerset Scrumpy Chicken

Scrumpy is the name given to cider that originates in the South West of England – the name is thought to come from the verb 'to scrump', which means to steal fruit! It is thanks to the generous addition of cider that this soup will have you 'ooohing' and 'aaahing' after just one spoonful!

Melt the butter in a large saucepan and sweat the onion for 20 minutes. Put a lid on the pan to help the slices steam a little. Add the grated apple and cook for a few minutes longer.

Stir in the flour and cook out for a few minutes, then gradually add the cider and cider vinegar. Cook for 1–2 minutes before adding the stock, slowly. Stir between ladlefuls to prevent lumps forming. Reserve 250ml of the stock.

Simmer, with a lid on, for 30 minutes, adding a little more stock if the soup starts to thicken.

Finally, add the cooked chicken and the milk, bring back to a simmer, then add the crème fraiche and season to taste.

6 SERVINGS

15 MINUTES PREPARATION

1 HOUR 15 MINUTES COOKING

50g butter
1 large onion, sliced
1 medium Cox's apple, grated
50g flour
500ml dry cider
90ml cider vinegar
1 litre chicken stock
300g cooked chicken, shredded
60ml milk
70g crème fraiche
Salt
Black pepper

Salcombe Crab

This well-seasoned crab soup has a real depth of flavour and makes a great dish to serve as a starter. More of a bisque than a chowder, this recipe uses Salcombe Bay crabs, which tend to be larger than most and full of flavoursome meat.

Melt the butter in a large saucepan and sweat the vegetables for 10 minutes.

Add the wine and the brandy to the pan and cook until the soup has reduced by half.

Add the anchovy essence and the stock, and simmer for 20 minutes. Blend the soup until smooth.

Add the crab, cream, lemon juice, cayenne pepper and seasoning. Warm the soup through, but don't allow it to boil. Serve immediately.

6 SERVINGS

10 MINUTES PREPARATION

1 HOUR COOKING

50g butter
1 large onion, chopped
2 sticks celery, chopped
2 cloves garlic, chopped
200ml white wine
25ml brandy or sherry
20ml anchovy essence
1 litre fish or shellfish stock
800g crab meat 50/50 white to brown, picked over to remove any shell
200ml double cream
½ lemon, juiced
Pinch cayenne pepper
Salt
Pepper

Southeast England

The South East is a diverse and unique area that features both sprawling countryside and vibrant cities – counties include East and West Sussex, Berkshire, Hampshire and Kent. The region is also known for its beauty spots, which include the North Downs and the Chiltern Hills, as well as its two stunning National Parks, the South Downs and the New Forest.

This area is steeped in history and was a gateway for an array of invaders, who left many famous landmarks in their wake, such as the walled city of Canterbury, Battle Abbey near Hastings and Rochester's citadel. The region has a rich maritime and fishing heritage, too – the shingle beach at the Stade, Hastings, is home to Europe's largest beach-launched fishing fleet.

In this chapter you will find recipes that are sure to tantalise your taste buds, bursting as they are with ingredients inspired by the region. Among the stars of the local produce are the Jersey Royal® potato, with its distinctive, sweet and summery flavour, and Test Valley smoked trout from Hampshire. The fish is cured in salt, air-dried and smoked over oak chippings in a brick kiln, using traditional methods that have changed little for centuries.

Watercress, Asparagus and Crayfish

Watercress is a star performer in so many ways and adds a beautiful peppery bite to this summer asparagus soup. Crayfish are plentiful along the southeastern shores so, for a treat, we've topped our soup with a generous handful. Go on… treat yourself.

Melt the butter in a large saucepan and sweat the onion and celery for 10 minutes.

Add the stock and simmer for 20 minutes, or until the onion and celery are soft.

Add the asparagus to the boiling soup and cook for 5 minutes.

Remove the soup from the heat, add the watercress and blend until smooth.

Add most of the crayfish, reserving just a few for garnish. Season and stir the soup. Bring back to a simmer, but not for too long or the crayfish will be tough. Garnish with the reserved crayfish and a sprig of watercress.

6 SERVINGS

10 MINUTES PREPARATION

30 MINUTES COOKING

50g butter
1 medium onion, chopped
1 stick celery, chopped
1.25 litres vegetable stock
400g asparagus, cut into 1cm lengths
40g watercress, plus extra for garnish
300g cooked crayfish
Salt
Pepper

Summer Lettuce with Pea and Dill

The soil in the South East is ideal for growing lettuce and peas and we've taken our inspiration for this soup from locally farmed vegetables. If you're lucky enough to find pea shoots, use these to garnish your soup instead of dill.

Melt the butter in a large saucepan and sweat the onion for 10 minutes.

Add the stock to the pan and bring to the boil. Add the peas, lettuce and dill, keeping a little dill back in case it's too strong. Cook for a further 5 minutes, then blend the soup until smooth.

Add the yoghurt to the soup, season, and blend again. Chill the soup – once cool, if it is too thick, add a little cold stock and blend again. Serve with a topping of yoghurt and garnish with dill.

6 SERVINGS

10 MINUTES PREPARATION

30 MINUTES COOKING

I HOUR CHILLING

60g butter

1 medium onion, finely chopped

1.1 litres vegetable stock

700g peas

400g cos lettuce, roughly chopped

10g dill, chopped

120ml natural yoghurt, plus additional for serving

Salt

Pepper

Few sprigs dill, for serving

Test Valley Smoked Trout, Horseradish and Peas

The beautiful Test Valley in Hampshire is renowned for its clean, fresh waters and the techniques used for smoking trout. This soup showcases the delicious flavour of the smoked trout with peas and dill. Finished with a dash of hot horseradish sauce, this is a warming soup to nourish the soul.

Melt the butter in a large saucepan and sweat the onion and celery for 10 minutes.

Add the cauliflower to the pan and pour in the stock. Cover, and simmer for 20 minutes.

Add the milk, bring up to a simmer, and blend. Add the peas, cook for a few minutes and blend again, making sure you keep a few flecks of green.

Add the horseradish, seasoning and trout to the soup and bring to a simmer. Finally, add the dill and serve.

6 SERVINGS

15 MINUTES PREPARATION

30 MINUTES COOKING

50g butter

1 medium onion, chopped

1 stick celery, chopped

1 large cauliflower, chopped

1 litre chicken stock

200ml milk

380g peas

2 teaspoons horseradish

400g smoked trout, flaked with any bones removed

Handful fresh dill, roughly chopped

Salt

White pepper

Isle of Wight Tomato Consommé with Cucumber Noodles

Cucumber noodles are the perfect thing to eat during the hot summer months – cool, light and refreshing. Use a spiral vegetable slicer to create the noodle effect. Inspired by the warmth and white sands on the Isle of Wight, this soup is perfect as a summer supper.

Throw the tomato quarters, fennel and celery into a food processor a little at a time. When they are finely chopped, tip into a large bowl.

Add the salt, Worcestershire sauce and chilli flakes to the bowl and leave to marinate for as long as you can – 3 hours minimum.

Cover the inside of a large colander with muslin cloth, then place over a large bowl. You'll need something between the bowl and the colander to keep them 15cm apart – a small upturned cereal bowl, perhaps.

Tip the marinated vegetables into the lined colander, cover with cling film and refrigerate overnight. Don't be tempted to push the liquid through the muslin.

The result is a lovely, fresh-tasting clear consommé (you can use the vegetable pulp to make tomato sauces, ragus or chutneys).

For the cucumber noodles, julienne the cucumber, sprinkle with salt and marinate for a few minutes. Drain off any liquid and tumble with the basil. Divide the cucumber noodles between the bowls and top each with chilled consommé.

6 SERVINGS

10 MINUTES PREPARATION

3 HOURS MARINATING

OVERNIGHT STRAINING

4kg ripe tomatoes, quartered
2 medium fennel, chopped
5 sticks celery, roughly chopped
1 tablespoon salt, plus extra for sprinkling
1 tablespoon Worcestershire sauce
Pinch chilli flakes
1 cucumber, peeled and deseeded
Handful basil leaves, finely shredded

Minted Nettles with Smashed Jersey Royals®

Delicious Jersey Royal® new potatoes, with their unique flavour from Jersey's fertile soil, combine with fresh nettles to create this dense and delicious dark green soup. Oozing with natural flavour, this unusual recipe is one that simply must be tried.

Put the Jersey Royals® in a large saucepan of salted water and cook, covered, for 20 minutes or until the potatoes are soft. Drain, return to the pan and cover again to keep the potatoes warm.

Heat the oil in a large saucepan and sauté the onion and leek for 10 minutes.

Add the chopped potato and the stock to the pan. Simmer, with a lid on, for 20 minutes, until the vegetables are soft.

While the soup is cooking, add the chives and the butter to the Jersey Royal® potatoes, and season. Smash the potatoes with a masher, leaving a good number of lumps – you're not making mash.

Add the nettle tops and mint to the soup. Season, and blend until smooth.

To serve, arrange a pile of crushed Jersey Royals® in the middle of a shallow soup plate and pour the nettle soup around the potato.

6 SERVINGS

10 MINUTES PREPARATION

30-40 MINUTES COOKING

400g Jersey Royals®, washed, with skins on
2 tablespoons olive oil
1 large onion, chopped
1 medium leek, chopped
1 large potato, chopped
1 litre vegetable stock
Handful chives, chopped
65g butter
260g nettle tops
Handful mint leaves
Salt
Pepper

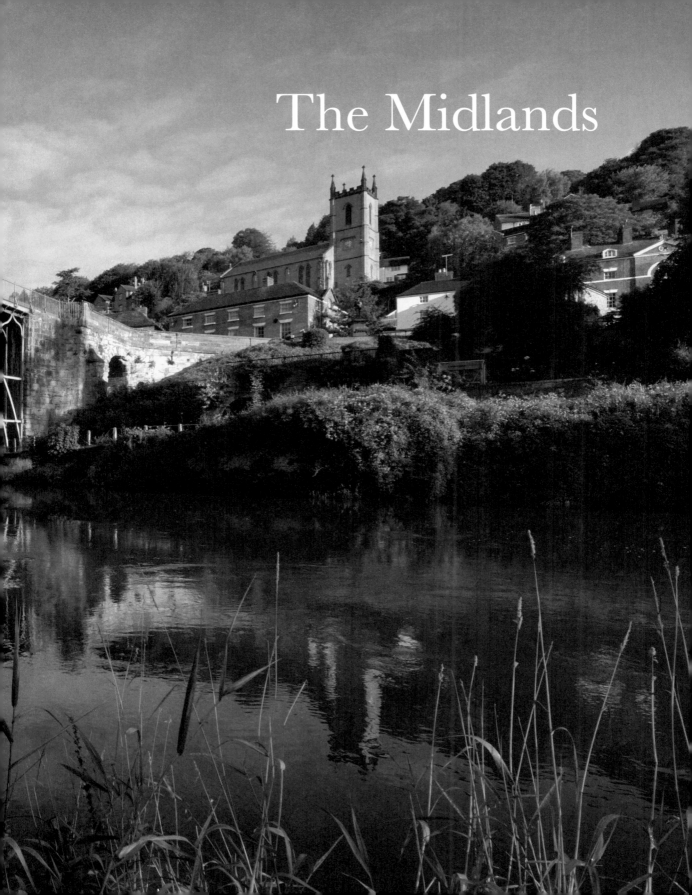

The Midlands

With the counties of Leicestershire, Lincolnshire and Northamptonshire to the east, and Staffordshire, Shropshire and Warwickshire to the west, the Midlands is an area spanning central England that broadly corresponds to the medieval kingdom of Mercia. Home to the Peak District National Park and the Cotswolds, the region has many breathtaking views, as well as an extensive system of romantic waterways and canals that is central to the area's industrial heritage of the 18th and 19th centuries.

At the centre of the region is Birmingham, a vibrant city with a world-class cultural scene. It is also home to Shakespeare! Renowned local foods such as Shropshire Fidget Pie and Malvern Pudding are still eaten regularly throughout the region. Our recipes from the Midlands maximise on local ingredients that include malty ales, orchard fruits and fine cheeses.

Burton Braised Beef

This soup was inspired by the long ale-making history of Brewers of Burton. Slow-cooked in ale, the ox cheeks soften beautifully, producing a lovely rich flavour. The celery, carrots and potato only add to the depth of flavour in this delicious recipe.

Preheat the oven to 160°C/gas mark 3.

Heat the oil in a large saucepan and brown the ox cheeks, turning to colour evenly. Remove the meat from the pan and set aside.

In the same saucepan, brown the onion wedges for 5 minutes. Add the garlic, if using, tomato purée and bay. Return the meat to the pan.

Add the ale, the stock or water and the Worcestershire sauce to the pan. Season, and bring to a simmer. Transfer the soup to an ovenproof dish and place in the oven for 4 hours, or until the ox cheeks are starting to fall apart.

Add the remaining ingredients to the dish and cook for a further 40 minutes. Remove the bay leaf from the soup before serving.

6 SERVINGS

20 MINUTES PREPARATION

5 HOURS COOKING

4 tablespoons oil

1kg ox cheeks, cut into 3cm chunks

1 large onion, cut into chunky wedges

2 cloves garlic (optional)

2 tablespoons tomato purée

1 bay leaf

550ml ale

1 litre brown beef stock or water

2 tablespoons Worcestershire sauce

2 sticks celery, diced

1 large Maris Piper potato, diced

2 large carrots, diced

Salt

Coarse black pepper

Shropshire Blue Cheese, Cauliflower and Pear

Midlands' dairies have been making blue cheeses for hundreds of years. Using Colston Bassett's Shropshire Blue, this is our version of a recipe that has been handed down through many generations. It makes a creamy soup with wonderful flavour.

Melt the butter in a large saucepan and sweat the onion, garlic, leek and celery for 10 minutes. Add the pear cider and cook for 2 minutes.

Heat the stock in a separate pan then add to the soup, together with the cauliflower, pears and apple juice. Simmer for 20 minutes, until the vegetables and pears are soft. Blend the soup.

Add two-thirds of the cheese and the crème fraiche to the soup, season and blend.

Before serving the soup, top each bowl with a sprinkling of the remaining cheese.

6 SERVINGS

20 MINUTES PREPARATION

35 MINUTES COOKING

30g butter
1 medium onion, diced
1 clove garlic, diced
1 medium leek, sliced
2 sticks celery, sliced
100ml pear cider
1 litre vegetable stock
1 large cauliflower, roughly chopped
3 medium ripe pears,
cut into chunks
80ml apple juice
160g Colston Bassett Shropshire
Blue cheese
40g crème fraiche
Salt
White pepper

Evesham Asparagus Risotto with Berkswell Cheese

The Vale of Evesham is renowned for asparagus and we have teamed it with a favourite hard sheep's cheese of ours, called Berkswell. Very moreish, this cheese tastes sweet and dry – similar to an Italian pecorino – and adds an amazing tangy flavour to the mix.

Place the asparagus in a large saucepan of rapidly boiling salted water and cook for 1–2 minutes, depending on size. Refresh in cold water and drain.

Chop three-quarters of the asparagus, and blend the rest to a smooth green purée with a little cold stock. Reserve for later.

Heat the oil in a large saucepan and sweat the onion, celery, fennel and garlic for 10 minutes.

Add the stock and potato to the pan and simmer for 20 minutes, or until all the vegetables are cooked. Blend until very smooth.

Add the rice to the soup and cook until the rice has softened. This will take approximately 20 minutes.

Add the chopped asparagus, asparagus purée, two-thirds of the Berkswell cheese and the single cream. Stir everything into the soup and warm for 5 minutes.

Finally, add the lemon zest and spring onions, season and serve topped with the remaining cheese.

6 SERVINGS

20 MINUTES PREPARATION

40 MINUTES COOKING

450g asparagus
1.3 litres vegetable stock
50ml olive oil
1 large onion, finely diced
3 sticks celery, finely diced
1 medium fennel, sliced
2 cloves garlic, crushed
1 medium potato, chopped
100g risotto rice
90g Berkswell cheese (or another hard sheep's cheese), finely grated
55ml single cream
1 lemon, zested
4 spring onions, sliced
Salt
Black pepper

Lightly Spiced Parsnip and Bramley Apple

The first recorded Bramley tree grew from pips that a young girl planted in her garden in Southwell, Nottinghamshire, in 1909. Today the apple is known as the King of Covent Garden. How could we ignore an ingredient with such great British heritage? Blended with gentle spices, parsnips and cream, the tart fruit makes a heavenly soup.

Melt the butter in a large saucepan and sweat the onion and celery for 10 minutes. Add the garlic, if using, and cook for 2 minutes more.

Add the spices to the pan, together with the apple and parsnip. Cook for 5 minutes.

Pour in the vegetable stock and simmer until all the vegetables are soft. This should take about 20 minutes.

Add the cream and lemon juice to the soup, season and blend before serving.

6 SERVINGS

10 MINUTES PREPARATION

40 MINUTES COOKING

60g butter
½ large onion, diced
2 sticks celery, chopped
1 clove garlic, chopped (optional)
Good pinch ground cumin
Good pinch garam masala
Pinch cayenne pepper
1 large Bramley apple, chopped
6 large parsnips, chopped
1.2 litres vegetable stock
120ml double cream
½ lemon, juiced
Salt
White pepper

Pea and Mint with Crème Fraiche

Crème fraiche provides a tang that sets this soup apart from its peers. It also makes the perfect accompaniment to sweet spring peas, onion and mint. This soup can be eaten hot, but works equally well served chilled on a warm summer's day.

Heat the oil in a large saucepan and sweat the onion until it is translucent in colour, about 10 minutes.

Add the vegetable stock to the pan, along with the potato, and simmer for 20 minutes or until the vegetables are cooked. Season.

Add the peas and the mint leaves. Cook for 5 minutes, then add the crème fraiche and blend the soup. Check the seasoning and add more mint if desired.

6 SERVINGS

10 MINUTES PREPARATION

30 MINUTES COOKING

50ml rapeseed oil

1 medium onion, chopped

1.2 litres vegetable stock

1 large potato, chopped

700g peas

10 mint leaves, plus extra to garnish (optional)

100g crème fraiche

Salt

White pepper

Shropshire Pea, Mint and Spinach

Smooth and vibrant, this sumptuous soup is a twist on a British favourite. This classic English soup uses the simple pea, sweet and delicious. Here, the spinach adds a velvety texture to the soup, which is further enriched with mint and fresh cream.

6 SERVINGS

10 MINUTES PREPARATION

30 MINUTES COOKING

50g butter

1 medium onion, finely chopped

1 stick celery, finely chopped

1 large Maris Piper potato, cut into small pieces

1 litre vegetable stock

750g fresh peas

200g spinach

Few mint leaves

180ml single cream

Salt

Pepper

Melt the butter in a large saucepan and sweat the onion and celery until soft.

Add the potato and stock and simmer for 20 minutes, or until the potato is soft.

Add 600g of the peas and cook for 5 minutes – any longer and you will lose the colour from the peas.

Add the spinach, mint and cream to the pan. Blend the soup, adding more stock or water to reach the desired thickness. Season to taste.

Cook the remaining peas for 5 minutes in boiling water and add to the soup just before serving.

Eastern
England

A large proportion of our soup is made in Peterborough, making the East our heartland. This is Britain's lowest-lying region, with over 50 per cent of its borders made up of coastline. Pretty inland villages with tulip and daffodil farms typify this region, as do coastal fishing towns with stretches of sandy beaches. Counties include Suffolk, Norfolk, Bedfordshire, Cambridgeshire, Essex and Hertfordshire.

Cromer crab is one of this region's most famous foods. Associated with the eponymous coastal town in Norfolk, these crabs are smaller and sweeter than elsewhere, and thrive on the chalk reef just off the coast. The region is also known for its big and juicy Brancaster mussels. Then, of course, there are turkeys. The flat, fertile plains of Norfolk provide the ideal habitat for rearing these birds, which, a century ago, were walked to London for the Christmas markets.

For the recipes in this section we have made the most of the produce from the region's nutrient-rich, arable farmland. Fenland celery has a delicate, sweet, nutty taste and a clean, crisp texture, both of which owe much to the traditional growing methods used and the rich, Fenland soil in which it grows. It is in the low-lying county of Norfolk that asparagus is said to be at its best. Light, sandy soils and fluctuating temperatures result in asparagus of the highest quality, with great British taste and flavour.

Tudor's East Anglian Spicy Roast Butternut Squash

East Anglia has long been known for its vegetables – especially potatoes – and sugar crops. Today the fertile flatlands of East Anglia provide a much larger variety of vegetables, including squash. This silky smooth combination of butternut squash and herbs is technical officer Tudor Darie's idea of bliss. Vibrant and warming, the recipe is testimony to his expertise.

Preheat the oven to 200°C/gas mark 6.

Put the squash in a large bowl and add the chilli flakes, fennel seeds and thyme. Add 4 tablespoons of the olive oil and mix to coat everything evenly. Transfer to a baking tray, scraping any residue from the bowl. Place the baking tray in the oven and roast the squash until soft and coloured, 40–45 minutes.

Heat the remaining olive oil in a large, heavy-bottomed saucepan. When hot add the sage leaves and sauté for 30 seconds, until crispy. Remove and set aside.

Add the onions, carrots and garlic to the pan and sweat until the onions are translucent. Add the paprika and stir to coat the vegetables. Add the stock and bring to the boil, then simmer until the vegetables are soft. Remove from the heat.

When the cooked squash is cool enough to handle, scoop out the flesh and add to the soup. Bring the soup back to the boil and cook for 2–3 minutes.

Remove from the heat, then blend the soup until smooth and creamy.

Stir in the Parmesan, season to taste with salt and pepper and serve garnished with crispy sage leaves.

6–8 SERVINGS

10 MINUTES PREPARATION

1 HOUR COOKING

2 medium butternut squash, cubed with skin on
1 teaspoon dried chilli flakes
2 teaspoons dried fennel seeds
Small handful fresh thyme
6 tablespoons olive oil
Small handful fresh sage leaves
2 medium onions, chopped
3 carrots, sliced
3 cloves garlic, chopped
1 teaspoon paprika
1 litre chicken or vegetable stock
50g grated Parmesan
Salt
Pepper

Louise's Lincolnshire Pumpkin

This wholesome pumpkin soup is the creation of Louise Willis, our regional human resources specialist. It works just as well as a weeknight meal or an elegant starter for your guests. Silky smooth with a velvety texture, this autumn favourite is enhanced by the warming tones of nutmeg.

Preheat the oven to 200°C/gas mark 6.

Place the pumpkin in a roasting dish with the onion and the carrots. Coat the vegetables in the rapeseed oil and roast until the pumpkin is soft, around 40 minutes.

Pour the stock into a large saucepan and add the celery, potato and leek. Bring to the boil, then simmer lightly until the potato is soft, around 15 minutes.

Add the roasted pumpkin, onion and carrot to the pan and simmer for a further 10 minutes.

Remove the pan from the heat and blend the soup until smooth and creamy. Add seasoning and the nutmeg.

Finally, stir in the cream and sherry, and serve hot with a crusty cob.

6-8 SERVINGS

15 MINUTES PREPARATION

45 MINUTES COOKING

1 medium pumpkin, cut into chunks
1 medium onion, chopped
2 medium carrots, chopped
2 tablespoons rapeseed oil
1.2 litres chicken stock
3 sticks celery, sliced
1 large floury potato, cubed
1 small leek, sliced into rings
1½ teaspoons ground nutmeg
250ml double cream
50ml sherry
Salt
Pepper

Fenland Celery and Stilton

This is a smooth, deeply satisfying winter soup. Fenland celery is in season from late October to December and is much paler than regular green celery. It tastes a little sweeter, too, and has a nutty flavour. The Stilton gives the soup a slightly tangy finish.

Melt the butter in a large saucepan and sweat the onion, leek and celery for a good 15 minutes – they should be translucent in colour. Add the garlic and cook for a further 2 minutes.

Add the celeriac, followed by the stock. Put a lid on the pan and simmer for 20–30 minutes. When all the vegetables are soft, blend the soup until smooth, adding a little more stock if you need it.

Finally, stir in the cream and the Stilton, and season to taste. Blend the soup again. If you like, reserve some of the Stilton before blending and sprinkle it over the soup before serving. That way you will have some lovely melty bits.

6 SERVINGS

10 MINUTES PREPARATION

50 MINUTES COOKING

50g unsalted butter
1 medium onion, finely chopped
1 medium leek, sliced
1 head celery, sliced
2 cloves garlic, finely chopped
1 medium to large celeriac, finely diced
1.2 litres vegetable stock
70ml double cream
150g Stilton, crumbled
Salt
White pepper

Albany's Roast Chicken and Parsnip

Our new-product development manager Albany Ward has created this scrumptious roast dinner soup. She uses Lincolnshire Poacher, a delicious local cheese with a deep, complex flavour and a smooth lingering aftertaste – often with a hint of sweetness. Rich and indulgent, this soup is sure to make it onto your list of favourites.

Melt the butter in a large saucepan and add the garlic, parsnips and potatoes. Stir until everything has an even coating of butter.

Pour in the chicken stock and boil until the potatoes and parsnips are cooked.

Stir in the cheese and the roast chicken, then blend the soup until smooth. For a silkier finish, pass the blended soup through a sieve.

Stir in the double cream and lemon juice.

Return to a low heat for 5 minutes.

Season to taste and serve.

4 SERVINGS

10 MINUTES PREPARATION

30 MINUTES COOKING

25g butter
3 cloves garlic, crushed
200g parsnips, diced
200g potatoes, diced
450ml chicken stock
30g Lincolnshire Poacher cheese, grated
80g cooked roast chicken, shredded
2 tablespoons double cream
1 teaspoon lemon juice
Salt
White pepper

Cromer Crab Bisque

Smaller and sweeter than other varieties, the Cromer crab has played a seasonal role (March to October) in the Norfolk way of life for centuries. A steaming crab bisque is very welcome on a cold day – our version of this traditional culinary delight will not disappoint.

Melt the butter in a large saucepan and sweat the onion, celery, carrot and fennel for 10 minutes. Add the garlic and cook for a further 2 minutes.

Add the tomato purée, smoked paprika, sherry and vermouth, and cook for 5 minutes.

Pour the stock into the pan and the chopped tomatoes and herbs. Simmer for 20 minutes with a lid on. When all the vegetables are nice and soft, remove the bay and parsley and blend the soup until smooth.

Add the cream and blend again.

Finally, stir in the crab and add cayenne pepper, lemon juice and seasoning to taste. Bring the soup back up to temperature and serve immediately.

6 SERVINGS

10 MINUTES PREPARATION

40 MINUTES COOKING

50g butter
1 large onion, finely diced
2 sticks celery, finely diced
1 large carrot, finely diced
½ medium fennel, finely diced
3 cloves garlic, crushed
100g tomato purée
1 teaspoon smoked paprika
100ml sherry
100ml vermouth or white wine
1 litre shellfish stock
200g tinned chopped tomatoes
1 bay leaf
2–3 parsley stalks
130ml double cream
300g white crabmeat
Pinch cayenne pepper
½ lemon, juiced
Salt
White pepper

Louise's Split Pea

Louise Willis's chunky, spicy soup makes a perfect
weekday meal. Low in calories and extremely
nutritious, the recipe is also a winner with the health-
conscious among us. Blend the soup if you prefer a
smooth finish, and top with a dollop of crème fraiche
for a little added richness.

Put all of the ingredients in a slow cooker or heavy-
bottomed saucepan and simmer for 4 hours, until the
peas are soft.

Remove the bay leaves before serving.

8 SERVINGS

15 MINUTES PREPARATION

4 HOURS COOKING

250g dried green split peas
1.2 litres vegetable stock
2 medium potatoes, chopped
2 sticks celery, chopped
2 medium carrots, sliced
1 medium onion, diced
2 cloves garlic, minced
1 teaspoon dry mustard
1 teaspoon ground cumin
1 teaspoon chopped sage
1 teaspoon chopped thyme
3 bay leaves
Salt
Pepper

Stiffkey Cockles with Bacon and Spinach

Stiffkey cockles are sometimes known as Stewkey blues, owing to the pale lavender to dark grey-blue colour of their shells. It comes from their habitat a few centimetres beneath mud and sand. Any clams or mussels can be used in their place. The addition of smoked bacon and spinach makes this recipe reminiscent of a chowder.

Heat the oil in a large saucepan and sauté the lardons until crispy. Remove from the pan using a slotted spoon and reserve on kitchen paper.

Using the same pan, heat the butter and sweat the onion for 5 minutes, then add the sage and potato.

Add the milk and stock slowly, keeping a little of the stock back. Cover and simmer for 20 minutes.

When the potatoes are soft, add the cooked bacon, chopped clams (or mussels), cream, spinach, paprika, and parsley. Season to taste and serve.

6 SERVINGS

10 MINUTES PREPARATION

30 MINUTES COOKING

20ml oil

150g smoked bacon lardons

50g butter

1 large onion, chopped

1 sage leaf

1 large floury potato (King Edwards work well), diced

500ml milk

600ml fish or ham stock

250g cooked clam meat (or mussel meat), chopped

50ml single cream

200g baby spinach, roughly chopped

Pinch smoked paprika

Handful flat-leaf parsley, roughly chopped

Salt

Coarse black pepper

Brancaster Mussel Stew

Brancaster mussels are collected from the sea when young and moved to lays in tidal creeks. Big, tender and juicy, they have unbeatable flavour. Tossed into a luxurious, creamy combination, they make a simply awesome soup. Sup and see for yourself.

Melt the butter in a large saucepan and sweat the onion, carrot and celery for 10 minutes. Add the chilli and garlic, then sweat for a further 2–3 minutes.

Add the stock and herbs and simmer for 10 minutes, then add the new potatoes and simmer for a further 15 minutes. Take care not to overcook the potatoes.

Meanwhile, cook the mussels. Place a large, dry saucepan over a high heat. When hot, throw in the mussels quickly followed by the wine. Cover, leave for 1 minute, then shake the pan. Leave for a few more minutes, still with the lid on.

Once all the mussels have opened, drain them in a colander, reserving the liquid. Remove the meat from the shells and strain the cooking juices through a fine sieve. If the mussels are a bit big, halve them, and discard any whose shells don't open.

When the potatoes are just about cooked, add the cream and the juices from the mussels to the soup and bring to a rolling boil in order to reduce the soup to a nice consistency.

Throw the mussels into the soup along with the parsley, lemon juice, paprika and seasoning. Remove the herbs, and sprinkle the soup with fresh thyme before serving.

6 SERVINGS

20 MINUTES PREPARATION

30–40 MINUTES COOKING

25g butter
1 large onion, thinly sliced
1 large carrot, thinly sliced
3 sticks celery, thinly sliced
½ medium red chilli, finely chopped
3 cloves garlic, crushed
800ml fish stock
1 bay leaf
2 sprigs thyme, plus extra for sprinkling
150g new potatoes, quartered (Charlottes are a good choice)
1.5kg fresh mussels
260ml white wine
260ml double cream
Good handful parsley, chopped
½ lemon, juiced
1 teaspoon paprika
Salt
White pepper

Norfolk Turkey

Lean, healthy and versatile, turkey is a great food for any time of year, and not just for using as leftovers after Christmas. We have combined this lean meat with a medley of market-garden vegetables. It's a simple recipe for a warming winter treat.

Melt the butter in a large saucepan and sweat the vegetables for 10 minutes. Add the garlic and cook for a further 2 minutes.

Add the bay leaf, then the flour, and cook for a further 3–4 minutes.

Slowly add the stock and the white wine, stirring as you go. Keep some stock back, depending on how thick you like the soup.

Add the potato and cook until soft, about 20 minutes.

Finally, add the turkey, mustard, spring greens and cream. Season to taste and cook for a further 10 minutes. Remove the bay leaf before serving.

6 SERVINGS

15 MINUTES PREPARATION

30–40 MINUTES COOKING

55g butter

1 medium onion, finely chopped

1 large leek, diced into 1cm rounds

2 sticks celery, finely chopped

1 large carrot, cut into 1cm chunks

2 cloves garlic, crushed

1 bay leaf

1 tablespoon flour

1 litre turkey or chicken stock

140ml white wine or cider

1 large Maris Piper or other waxy potato, diced into 2cm cubes

350g cooked turkey meat, shredded

2 teaspoons whole-grain mustard

100g spring greens, roughly chopped and blanched in boiling water

80ml single cream

Salt

Coarse black pepper

Asparagus and Samphire

Otherwise known as 'sea asparagus', Norfolk samphire makes the perfect addition to this soup. It thrives in the tidal salt marshes and the saltwater contributes to its fabulous flavour. Asparagus is also local, making this soup eastern England at its best.

Melt the butter in a large saucepan and sweat the onion, celery and leeks for 10 minutes.

Add the cauliflower and pour in the stock. Cook for 20 minutes, or until all the vegetables are soft. Blend the soup until very smooth.

Cut the spears from the tops of the asparagus and reserve. Cut the remaining stems into 1cm rounds. Add these rounds to the soup and cook for 5 minutes.

Season, add the crème fraiche or yoghurt and blend the soup again.

Finally, blanch the asparagus tips and samphire in unsalted boiling water for 2 minutes. Drain and pan-fry in a little butter. Stir in the lemon zest and use to garnish the soup before serving.

6 SERVINGS

20 MINUTES PREPARATION

40 MINUTES COOKING

50g butter, plus knob for frying
½ large onion, chopped
1 stick celery, chopped
2 medium leeks, chopped
1 small cauliflower, cut into florets
800ml vegetable stock
450g asparagus
100g crème fraiche or natural yoghurt
Good pinch salt
Pinch white pepper
40g samphire, chopped
½ lemon, zested

Northwest
England

The North West is a region of contrast – from the contemporary, cosmopolitan vibe of Manchester and the cultural and architectural grandeur of Liverpool to the Roman and medieval heritage of Chester, the rolling hills of Lancashire and the stunning scenery around the Lake District. This region has something for everyone, not least a long tradition of speciality dishes and local delicacies.

In this section you will find tempting recipes based on the North West's fantastic local produce, such as the Bury Black Pudding, which has roots dating back to the 1800s. One of our oldest British cheeses is Cheshire – it is even listed in the Domesday Book – which is perfect for crumbling into a hot soup. Cumberland sausages, once local fare, are now popular everywhere in Great Britain, as is Lancashire hotpot, the reputation and fame of which has travelled far and wide. 'Scouser', a term used to describe people from Liverpool, originates from the Lobscouse (or Scouse for short), a recipe that features in the following pages.

Broccoli and Lancashire Cheese

Lancashire cheese is made by blending curds of varying maturity. Not only does it lend a distinctive character when coupled with broccoli and spinach, it helps create a soup packed with vitamins and fibre. Add some Rarebit Croutons (see page 20) for that final touch, substituting Lancashire for the Cheddar.

Prepare the broccoli: trim the florets from the stalks, finely chop the stalks and put to one side, then roughly chop the florets, or pulse-blend in a food processor. This will help the broccoli to cook more quickly when added later, thus keeping the soup greener.

Melt the butter in a large saucepan and sweat the broccoli stalks, onion, celery and leek for 15 minutes. Cover with a lid between stirs.

Pour in the stock and bring to the boil. Simmer gently for 20 minutes. When the vegetables are cooked, especially the broccoli stalks, add the broccoli florets. Cook for a further 6–7 minutes. Finally, add the spinach and blend until very smooth. Season to taste.

To finish off, distribute the Lancashire cheese between the soup bowls, and ladle over the piping-hot soup. Give each bowl a stir and watch as the cheese starts to melt into the soup.

6 SERVINGS

15 MINUTES PREPARATION

40 MINUTES COOKING

2 large heads broccoli (about 650g in total, including the stalks)
50g butter or 50ml oil
½ large onion, chopped
2 sticks celery, chopped
1 medium leek, sliced
1 litre vegetable stock
150g baby leaf spinach
300g Lancashire cheese, crumbled
Salt
Pepper

Roasted Roots with Black Pudding Crumb

Bury, in Greater Manchester, produces the most famous variety of black pudding, using traditional methods that date back to the 19th century. And black puddings from Bury win international awards. In this unique soup, the black pudding is paired with sweet, juicy root vegetables. It's a perfect match.

Preheat the oven to 180°C/gas mark 4.

Roll the swede, parsnips and carrots in 2 dessertspoons of the oil, and season with salt and pepper. Spread the vegetables evenly over a roasting tray and roast in the oven for 30 minutes.

Melt the butter in a large saucepan and sweat the onion and celery for 10 minutes, until soft.

Add the chicken stock, the roasted root vegetables and a little seasoning. Cover, and simmer for 30 minutes.

Add the cream and blend the soup. If it is a bit thick, add a little water or more stock – it can vary depending on the sizes of vegetables. Adjust the seasoning.

To make the black pudding crumb, place the ingredients in a food processor and pulse-blend to a chunky crumb. Spread the crumb out over a baking tray and bake in the oven for 15 minutes.

Ladle the soup into bowls and top with the black pudding crumb. Sprinkle with a little parsley before serving, if desired.

6 SERVINGS
30 MINUTES PREPARATION
1 HOUR 10 MINUTES COOKING

1 medium swede (about 400g), cut into 2cm chunks

3 large parsnips, chopped

2 large carrots, chopped

20ml oil

30g butter

1 medium onion, diced

1 stick celery, cut into chunks

1.5 litres chicken stock

2 tablespoons single cream

Chopped parsley (optional), for serving

FOR THE CRUMB

140g sliced bread

250g black pudding, peeled and diced

Salt

Pepper

Scouse

Scouse is a popular Merseyside dish, somewhat like a mixture of Irish stew and a Scandinavian dish called *lobscaus*. Full of flavour, this is a delicious lamb stew and is perfect served with bread and butter.

Preheat the oven to 160°C/gas mark 3.

Roll the lamb in the flour. Heat the oil in a large casserole dish and brown off the meat a little at a time. Using a slotted spoon, remove the meat from the dish and set aside.

Sauté the onion and carrots in the same dish, using a high heat to colour the vegetables slightly.

Return the lamb to the dish and pour in the lamb stock. Season with salt and pepper, and add the Worcestershire sauce. Cover, and cook in the oven for 2 hours.

Add the potatoes to the casserole dish and cook for another hour, until the potatoes start to break down and thicken the soup. Add a little more Worcestershire sauce, if needed, and season again, before serving.

---

6 SERVINGS

30 MINUTES PREPARATION

3 HOURS COOKING

800g lamb neck, cut into 3cm chunks

2 tablespoons flour

40ml oil

1 large onion, cut into chunky wedges

3 large carrots, diced

1.5 litres lamb stock

2 tablespoons Worcestershire sauce, plus extra to taste (optional)

800g potatoes, cut into large chunks

Salt

Coarse black pepper

Lancashire Hotpot

Is it possible to improve on the simple perfection of the Lancashire hotpot? See for yourself, with our twist on the original culinary creation. Perfect for a hearty, warming meal, why not serve this soup with our Crispy Wedges (see page 20)?

Preheat the oven to 170°C/gas mark 3.

Roll the lamb in the flour with some salt and pepper, shaking off any excess. Heat the oil in a large frying pan and brown off the meat. Don't overcrowd the pan, the meat will fry better if each chunk has a little space around it. Brown on one side before turning – you'll get better colour.

Remove the meat from the pan using a slotted spoon, and place in an ovenproof saucepan. Using the same frying pan, fry the onion for a few minutes to get some colour. Add to the lamb and repeat with the carrot.

Add the herbs and the stock, season and cook in the oven for 1 hour 30 minutes. The meat should be breaking apart.

Before serving the soup, remove the herbs and adjust the seasoning to taste.

6 SERVINGS

20 MINUTES PREPARATION

2 HOURS COOKING

900g lamb neck fillet, cut into 3cm chunks

2 tablespoons plain flour

20ml oil

1 large onion, cut into thick half slices

2 large carrots, cut into large chunks

1 bay leaf

3 sprigs thyme

1 litre lamb stock

Salt

Black pepper

Cumberland Sausage and Beans

Cumberland was once a northwestern county in its own right, but now makes up part of Cumbria. The eponymous sausage is a long, lightly spiced, rough-chopped-pork affair, usually sold coiled around itself. Traditionally, Cumberland sausages were sold by length rather than weight – they could be over a metre long! Bolstered with a medley of beans, this hearty soup will warm you on a cold day.

Preheat the oven to 200°C/gas mark 6.

Heat the oil in a large saucepan and sweat the onion and the carrots for 10 minutes, then add the garlic and cook for a further minute.

Stir in the spices and cook for 1 minute. Add the red wine vinegar, Worcestershire sauce and tomato purée, and cook for a further 2 minutes.

Add all the remaining ingredients, except the sausage and seasoning, and simmer the soup for 30 minutes. When the vegetables are cooked, remove a ladle or two of the soup, blend a little, and return to the pan. Now add seasoning.

Squeeze the meat from the sausage skins, roll into balls about the size of cherries and place on a baking tray. Bake in the oven for 10 minutes.

Drain any oil from the sausage balls before spooning them into soup bowls, and pour the soup over the sausage balls to serve.

6 SERVINGS

20 MINUTES PREPARATION

50 MINUTES COOKING

2 tablespoons oil

1 large onion, chopped

2 large carrots, chopped

2 cloves garlic, crushed

2 teaspoons smoked paprika

Good pinch cumin seeds

1 tablespoon red wine vinegar

1 tablespoon Worcestershire sauce

50g tomato purée

1 litre chicken stock

200g tinned chopped tomatoes

150g tinned haricot or butter beans, drained

100g tinned black-eyed beans, drained

200g tinned cannellini beans, drained

1 teaspoon chopped fresh rosemary

33g dried red lentils

600g Cumberland sausage

Salt

Black pepper

Creamy Celeriac with Morecambe Bay Shrimps

This is a rich velvety soup complemented by the addition of the shrimps that are harvested in the wild and treacherous shifting sands of Morecambe Bay. Potted in nutmeg-flavoured butter, these sweet, brown shrimps are a local delicacy.

Melt 25g of butter in a large saucepan and sweat the onion and celery for 5 minutes. Add the celeriac and sweat for a further 10 minutes.

Pour in the white wine and vegetable stock and season with salt and white pepper. Cover, and simmer for 30 minutes, or until the celeriac is very soft. Add the single cream and blend until very smooth. Keep the soup warm while you cook the shrimps.

Drop the remaining butter into a hot frying pan and cook until the butter is hot and foaming. Just as it starts to turn brown, squeeze in a dash of lemon juice.

Throw in the shrimps, the chives, salt and black pepper. Cook for 2–3 minutes, until the shrimps turn pink and opaque. Ladle the soup into bowls and spoon the shrimps over the top, along with some of the hot flavoured butter.

6 SERVINGS

10 MINUTES PREPARATION

40 MINUTES COOKING

50g butter
1 medium onion, finely chopped
2 sticks celery, finely chopped
1 large celeriac, cut into 2cm chunks
200ml white wine
1 litre vegetable stock
100ml single cream
½ lemon, juiced
320g brown shrimps
Good pinch of chives
Salt
White pepper
Coarse black pepper

Manx Broth

Beef shin, leek, celery and turnip flavour this hearty broth from the Isle Of Man. Traditional fare at a Manx wedding feast, this broth used to be served in wooden bowls known as 'piggins' and supped with mussel shells, called 'sligs', for cutlery. We've updated the cutlery while maintaining the original essence of this tasty soup.

Place the beef in a large saucepan, pour in the stock and bring to the boil. Skim the surface and simmer for 2 hours uncovered. (Keeping topping up if the liquid reduces too much.)

Add the turnips, onion, carrots and celery, the barley and the thyme, and cook for another hour.

When the shin is starting to break apart, add the leeks and simmer the soup for another 10 minutes. Remove the thyme sprigs.

Finally, add the parsley and season.

6 SERVINGS

15 MINUTES PREPARATION

3-4 HOURS COOKING

600g beef shin, diced into 3cm pieces

2.5 litres beef stock

2 medium turnips, diced

1 large onion, diced

2 large carrots, diced

2 sticks celery, diced

100g dried pearl barley

2 sprigs thyme

1 large leek, diced into 2cm pieces

10g parsley, chopped

Salt

Black pepper

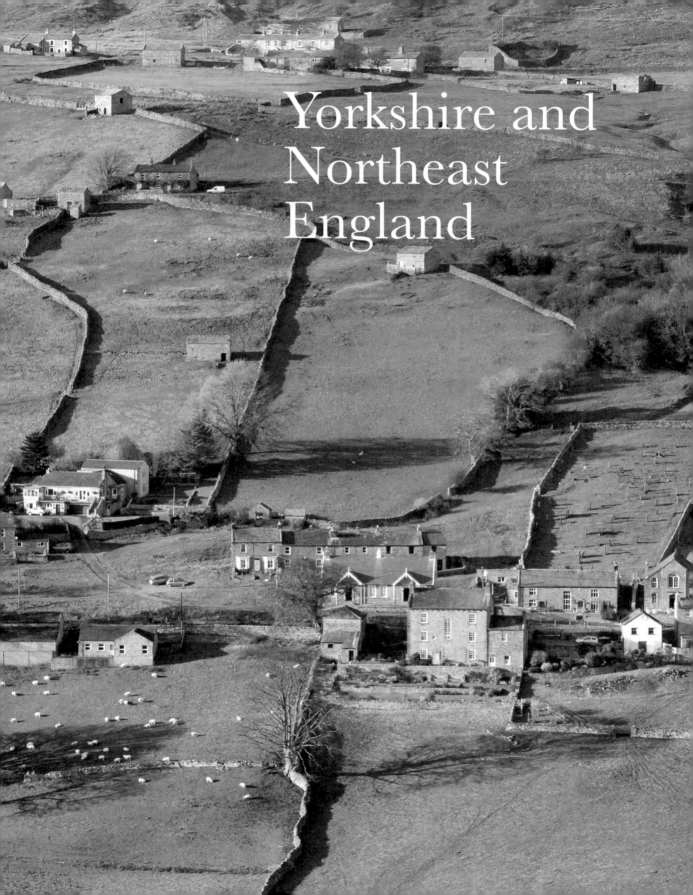

Yorkshire and Northeast England

Vast rolling Yorkshire moors, ancient castles, the rich natural beauty of miles of coastline and world-renowned landmarks that include Hadrian's Wall: these are hallmark features of Yorkshire and Northeast England.

Comprising the counties of Northumberland, Cleveland, Durham, Yorkshire and Tyne and Wear, this region has a number of special delicacies from which our recipes take inspiration. There are also many wonderful local ingredients that include the ales of the north, fish from the coastal waters and fine cheeses from Yorkshire.

The city of Newcastle has its own bread, the 'stottie', a flat circle of dough baked at the bottom of the oven for supreme softness. Herring caught in the North Sea and landed at Craster are said to make some of the finest kippers in the country, smoked for 16 hours in small stone smokehouses near the shore. Wensleydale, with its crumbly texture, was first made by monks who settled in the area. Today it remains one of the nation's favourite cheeses and is the backdrop for one of our delicious soups.

Pease Pudding with Saveloy

Pease pudding is a traditional British recipe hailing from the North East of England. Our version combines yellow split peas with salty saveloy sausages and ham stock. It is best served with Stottie Cakes (see page 24), unleavened bread that takes its name from the Geordie word 'stot', which means to bounce. The name refers to the dense texture of the dough, which, in theory, would cause the bread to bounce if dropped!

Melt the butter in a large saucepan and sweat the onion and the carrot for 10 minutes.

Add all the remaining ingredients (except the saveloy), cover with a lid and simmer for 1 hour, until the peas are totally soft. Remove the bay leaf and blend the soup. Add a touch more stock or water if needed.

Stir the sliced saveloy sausage into the soup and warm through before serving.

6 SERVINGS

10 MINUTES PREPARATION

1 HOUR 10 MINUTES COOKING

25g butter
1 large onion, chopped
1 large carrot, chopped
550g dried yellow split peas
1.2 litres ham or chicken stock
1 bay leaf
250g saveloy sausage, sliced
Salt
Pepper

Newcastle Brown Onion

This simple combination oozes flavour from both the onions and the world-famous Newcastle Brown Ale®. First brewed in 1927 for the hard-working people of the North East, the ale adds a delicate fruit aroma with caramel and brown sugar notes. The soup has a unique, nutty malt taste and is the perfect match for our Cheesy Croutes (see page 20).

Melt the butter in a large saucepan and sauté the onions for a good 20 minutes, until they are soft and evenly browned.

Add the sherry and cook for 5 minutes, before stirring in the flour. Cook for a further 5 minutes.

Slowly add the warm beef stock a little at a time, stirring constantly, then add the ale and the herbs.

Simmer, covered, for 30 minutes, and remove the herbs before serving.

6 SERVINGS

10 MINUTES PREPARATION

1 HOUR COOKING

50g butter

5 large onions, halved and finely sliced

25ml sherry

2 tablespoons flour

1.3 litres warm beef stock

400ml Newcastle Brown Ale®

1 bay leaf

4 sprigs thyme

Cauliflower, Broccoli and Yorkshire Wensleydale with Wild Garlic

Yorkshire Wensleydale cheese, lovingly handcrafted in the heart of the Yorkshire Dales, is creamy, crumbly and full of flavour. Here, it pairs beautifully with broccoli and cauliflower. In spring, wild garlic lines the banks of Northumberland's rivers. It is one of our favourite ingredients and adds yet another delicious taste dimension to this soup.

Melt the butter in a large saucepan and sweat the onion for 10 minutes. Add the flour and cook out for 2–3 minutes.

Add the cauliflower florets to the pan and pour in the stock. Simmer for 20 minutes, then blend.

Blanch the broccoli in salted water and add to the soup, along with cream cheese, half the Wensleydale and the wild garlic. Season and allow all the ingredients to warm through.

Pour the soup into heated bowls, and top with the remaining Wensleydale.

6 SERVINGS

15 MINUTES PREPARATION

30 MINUTES COOKING

60g butter

1 large onion, finely diced

1 tablespoon flour

1 large cauliflower, florets trimmed and chopped

900ml vegetable stock

2 heads broccoli (600g in total), florets trimmed

80g cream cheese

225g Wensleydale cheese, crumbled

3 wild garlic leaves, shredded

Salt

White pepper

Summer Allotment

Growing your own vegetables is a great British pastime, so we've kicked off our muddy boots and created this deliciously flavoured allotment soup. The wide variety of flavours from the vegetables fuse together to create this summer combination.

Heat the oil in a large saucepan and sauté the onion, carrots, fennel and celery for 10 minutes, then add the garlic.

Pour in the stock and the tinned tomatoes. Season and cover, then simmer for 15 minutes.

Add the cannellini beans, the courgette, the French beans and the peas. Simmer for 5 minutes.

Finally, stir in the spinach, check the seasoning and serve immediately.

6 SERVINGS

15 MINUTES PREPARATION

30 MINUTES COOKING

20ml olive oil

1 medium onion, chopped

2 medium carrots, chopped

½ medium fennel, halved and finely sliced

2 sticks celery, sliced

2 cloves garlic, sliced

1 litre vegetable stock

400g tinned chopped tomatoes

250g tinned cannellini beans, drained

1 large courgette, diced

150g French beans, cut into thirds

100g peas

150g baby spinach, roughly chopped

Salt

Black pepper

Winter Allotment

Make the most of your delicious winter vegetables by combining them in this great-tasting soup. We hope our allotment recipes are helpful to anyone growing their own vegetables, whether on a dedicated plot or at home in a kitchen garden. This recipe is sure to become a firm family favourite in no time.

Preheat the oven to 180°C/gas mark 4.

Roll the butternut squash, parsnips, sweet potato and carrots in the oil, season with salt and pepper, and spread the vegetables out evenly on a roasting tray. Roast in the oven for 30 minutes.

Melt the butter in a large saucepan and sweat the onion and the celery for 10 minutes, then add the roasted vegetables.

Pour in the stock, cover, and simmer for 30 minutes.

Add the cream and blend the soup. If the soup is a bit thick, add a little water or more stock.

6 SERVINGS

20 MINUTES PREPARATION

1 HOUR 10 MINUTES COOKING

1 large butternut squash, chopped
2 large parsnips, chopped
1 medium sweet potato, cut into chunks
2 large carrots, chopped
2 tablespoons oil
30g butter
1 medium onion, diced
1 stick celery, diced
1.2 litres vegetable stock
50ml single cream
Salt
Pepper

Beetroot with Yorkshire Rhubarb

The 'rhubarb triangle' is a significant area covering over 30 square miles across Leeds, Bradford and Wakefield. Rhubarb thrives in the wet and cold Yorkshire winters. It is low in fat, full of vitamins and minerals and packed with powerful antioxidants. Beetroot's earthy charm and ubiquitous, distinctive flavour make this a spectacular combination.

Heat the oil in a large saucepan and sauté the onion and celery for 10 minutes. Add the ginger and cook for a further 5 minutes.

Add the beetroot, rhubarb and honey. Season, pour in the stock and simmer for 20 minutes.

Remove any bones from the mackerel fillet. Pour the hot soup into warmed bowls and top with dollops of crème fraiche, the flaked mackerel and dill.

6 SERVINGS

10 MINUTES PREPARATION

30 MINUTES COOKING

50ml oil

1 large onion, finely diced

2 sticks celery, finely diced

Thumb-sized piece root ginger, finely diced

620g cooked beetroot (not pickled), peeled and cut into pieces

3 large sticks rhubarb (about 270g), cut into chunks

1 teaspoon honey

1.1 litres vegetable stock

4 cooked mackerel fillets, skin removed, flaked

100g crème fraiche

Handful dill, chopped

Salt

Black pepper

Wales

Wales has a strong tradition of living off the land that stretches back as far as the ancient Celts. Since that time the country has retained a distinct cultural identity and is officially bilingual: some 560,000 inhabitants speak Welsh. In the late 19th century, Wales acquired its popular image as the 'land of song', in part owing to the *eisteddfod* festival of literature, music and performance that has its origins in the 12th century. Today Wales is renowned for its male choirs.

This region steeped in history has an equally rich culinary tradition, much of it shaped by the country's natural resources: Welsh lamb, farmed on lush mountain valleys, is world-famous; the Welsh coastline is home to the mussel farms of Bangor and Anglesey oysters; there is the laverbread or 'Welshman's caviar', made from seaweed collected from the shores of the Gower; and we mustn't overlook the Welsh leek – an enduring symbol of Wales and the star of traditional recipes from the Glamorgan sausage to our own soup interpretation of Welsh cawl.

Braised Oxtail Broth with Dulse

This classic Welsh recipe has the tasty addition of dulse – a seaweed that is very common in UK waters. Ancient Celtic warriors ate dulse to prevent scurvy when on the march. You can buy dulse in dried or flaked form from many supermarkets. It has the appearance of reddish tea leaves and adds the most fantastic flavour to any soup.

Preheat the oven to 160°C/gas mark 3.

Heat the oil in a large saucepan and brown the pieces of oxtail on all sides. Remove to a deep casserole dish. In the same pan, sauté the onion, carrots, celery and garlic and add to the casserole with the oxtail.

Pour the red wine into the saucepan and use a wooden spoon to scrape any sediment from the bottom. Add this to the casserole, followed by the tomato purée, the herbs and just enough stock to cover the oxtail.

Put a lid on the casserole dish and place in the oven for 5 hours. Check every hour or so, to make sure the liquid still covers the oxtail, and add a little more stock or water if needed.

When the oxtail is falling from the bone, remove the meat to a plate using a slotted spoon. Skim any froth from the top of the stock, and add water if you like it thinner or a little cornflour if it's too thin.

When the oxtail has cooled enough to handle, about 20 minutes, strip all the meat from the bone and return to the casserole dish.

Add the dried dulse, season and warm gently for 5 minutes. Remove the herbs before serving.

6 SERVINGS

20 MINUTES PREPARATION

5 HOURS COOKING

40ml oil
1.2kg oxtail, trimmed and cut into even-sized pieces
1 large onion, chopped
3 medium carrots, chopped
2 sticks celery, sliced
2 cloves garlic, crushed
250ml red wine
50g tomato purée
2 bay leaves
3 sprigs thyme
1.8 litres beef stock or water
Cornflour (optional)
2 teaspoons dried dulse
Salt
Coarse black pepper

Lamb and Vegetable Cawl

Cawl is Welsh for 'soup' and this particular recipe dates back to the 14th century. As in other parts of the UK, recipes are often passed down through the generations. This one is very simple – a soup made from a cut of lamb stewed slowly with winter root vegetables. Historically this would have been made using a cauldron over an open fire.

Preheat the oven to 150°C/gas mark 2.

Heat the oil in an ovenproof dish and brown off the lamb, in two batches. Remove from the pan using a slotted spoon and reserve. In the same dish, brown the onion and celery, then the garlic. Season with salt and black pepper.

Add the stock and the herbs to the dish and bring to a simmer. Cover, and place in the oven for 1 hour.

Remove the soup from the oven and skim any froth from the surface. Add the carrots, swede and barley, and return to the oven, covered, for 1 hour.

Remove the soup from the oven again, add the leeks and cook for a further 10 minutes, until soft. Remove the herbs, check the seasoning and serve with the parsley sprinkled on top.

6 SERVINGS

30 MINUTES PREPARATION

2½ HOURS COOKING

20ml oil
550g lamb neck fillet, cut into 3cm chunks
1 medium onion, chopped
2 sticks celery, chopped
2 cloves garlic, crushed
1.5 litres chicken stock or water
1 bay leaf
3 sprigs thyme
3 large carrots, chopped
½ large swede, roughly chopped
40g dried pearl barley
1 large leek, chopped
Salt
Coarse black pepper
Good handful parsley, chopped, to serve

Leek, Chicken and Bacon Cawl

Cawl, pronounced to rhyme with owl, is a one-pot dish considered by many to be the national dish of Wales. Traditionally, it's a country soup with ingredients centred around meat. In medieval Wales, an absence of grain and most vegetables led to a dependence on meat. The only vegetables readily available at this time were leeks and cabbages.

Heat the oil in a large saucepan and sauté the onion and celery for a few minutes, until lightly caramelised, then add the garlic.

Pour the stock into the pan and add the carrots and herbs. Cover, and simmer for 20 minutes, until soft.

Add the cabbage and cook for 10 minutes, then add the leeks and cook until both have softened.

Finally, add the meat and peas and cook for a further 5 minutes. Remove the herbs before serving and sprinkle with parsley.

6 SERVINGS

20 MINUTES PREPARATION

40 MINUTES COOKING

20ml oil

1 medium onion, cut into small wedges

2 sticks celery, sliced

2 cloves garlic, finely chopped

1.2 litres ham or chicken stock

2 medium carrots, sliced

2 sprigs thyme

1 sage leaf

1 bay leaf

100g savoy cabbage, roughly chopped

1 large leek, cut into rounds

200g cooked chicken thighs, shredded

200g pulled ham hock

65g frozen peas

Good handful parsley, chopped, to serve

Welsh Leek and Caerphilly Cheese

According to legend, in battle against the Saxons, St David advised the Welsh to wear a leek in order to recognise fellow countrymen. It is believed that this was a key factor in securing a great victory. Today, leeks are still worn on St David's Day. Here, they are teamed with mild, crumbly Caerphilly cheese. Delicious served with our recipe for Rarebit Croutons (see page 20).

6 SERVINGS

10 MINUTES PREPARATION

40 MINUTES COOKING

50g butter
4 large leeks, cut lengthways and finely sliced
1 large floury potato, diced
1.2 litres vegetable stock
300g Caerphilly cheese, grated
50ml single cream
40g cream cheese
5 spring onions, finely chopped

Melt the butter in a large saucepan and sweat the leeks for 10 minutes.

Stir in the potatoes, add the stock and simmer for 20 minutes, until the potatoes are soft. You can blend the soup at this stage if you like, adding a little more stock or water if the soup is too thick.

Add the cheese, the cream, the cream cheese and the spring onions. Let the cheese melt a little before serving – the soup is delicious with its pockets of soft cheese.

Creamy Cockle 'n' Mussel Chowder with Sweet Potato

This recipe makes great use of mussels and cockles, both of which are plentiful along Welsh shores. Both have nuggets of sweet flesh and copious juices. Cockles were traditionally sold outside pubs, 'weighed' using a pint glass for lack of any scales. This remains the prevalent measure for selling shellfish to this day. The taste of this chowder really is hard to beat!

Melt the butter in a large saucepan and sweat the onion for 10 minutes, then add the garlic and sweat for a further 1–2 minutes.

Add two-thirds of the sweet potatoes, the sweetcorn and the stock and simmer for 20 minutes, or until all the vegetables are soft. Blend, then add the remaining sweet potato and simmer for 15 minutes, until soft.

To cook the shellfish, heat a dry pan until very hot. Drop in the shellfish, immediately followed by the wine. Cover quickly and shake the pan, then leave to steam for 3 minutes, or until all the shells have opened. Tip the shellfish into a colander, reserving the cooking juices. When cool enough to handle, remove the meat from the shells and chop roughly.

Add the spring onions to the soup, along with the cayenne pepper, lemon juice, chopped shellfish meat and cooking juices. Season to taste and bring back to a simmer. Serve sprinkled with the parsley.

6 SERVINGS

30 MINUTES PREPARATION

1 HOUR COOKING

60g butter

1 medium onion, roughly chopped

2 cloves garlic, crushed

4 medium sweet potatoes, peeled and cut into chunks

350g tinned sweetcorn, drained

1 litre fish or vegetable stock

1kg mussels, trimmed and the bad ones discarded

500g cockles

200ml white wine or cider

2 spring onions, chopped

Pinch cayenne pepper

½ lemon, juiced

Salt

Black pepper

Good handful flat-leaf parsley, roughly chopped, to serve

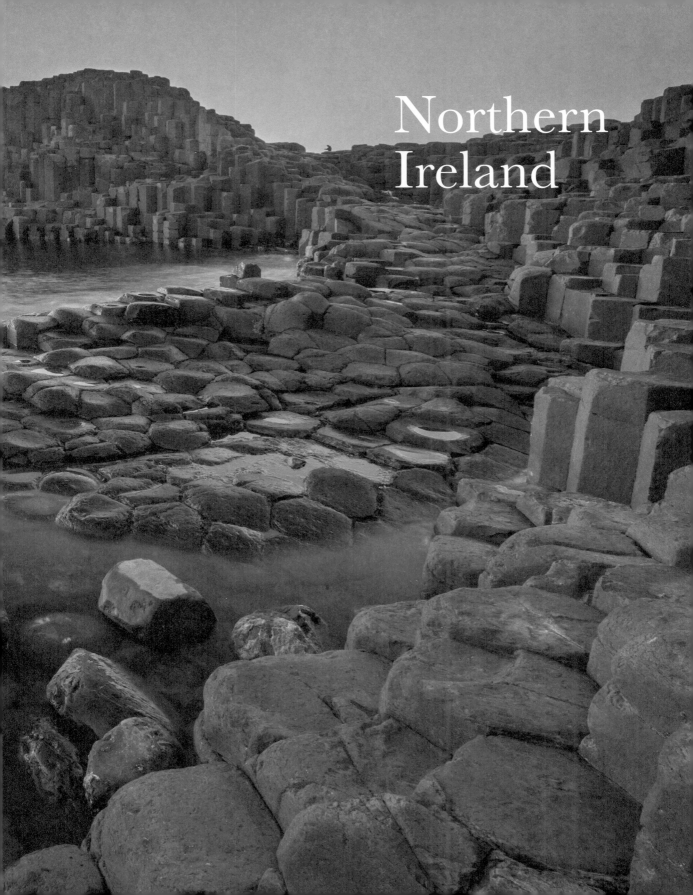

Northern Ireland

Ireland is the second largest of the British Isles. Incredibly green, this is a land of stunning sweeping vistas, in which rugged mountain ranges with cliff faces, crevices and underground caves dominate the skyline. The 17th March is St Patrick's Day, a national holiday. The saint is renowned for introducing Christianity to Ireland and on this day many wear a three-leafed shamrock – a metaphor for the Holy Trinity, and the national symbol of Ireland. Politically, this 'Emerald Isle' comprises the Republic of Ireland and Northern Ireland, which is part of the United Kingdom.

Northern Ireland's culinary heritage reflects a combination of Ulster-Scots and Irish traditions. Most dishes have their roots in potatoes and bread, the staples of bygone days. You can try a *blaa* (a soft white roll) in Waterford or snack on dulse (salty seaweed) in coastal areas. Other typical Irish foods include soda bread – every family in Ireland has its own recipe – and Irish stew. Traditionally made with mutton, onions and potatoes, this is stewed slowly for hours until the meat is tender.

Brotchan Roy

The word *roy* is derived from *ri*, the Irish word for king, so *brotchan roy* means 'broth fit for a king'. Exactly how far back this soup dates is debatable, with some claiming it's as old as the ancient druids. This recipe reflects the traditional way of making this soup – with leeks and oatmeal. Nowadays it is not uncommon to see potatoes in place of the oats.

Heat the milk and the stock in a large saucepan. As it warms sprinkle in the nutmeg and the oats. Simmer for 10 minutes.

Melt the butter in a separate saucepan and sweat the leeks for about 15 minutes, taking care not to let them colour. You can put a lid on the pan for a few minutes to help the leeks cook faster.

Add the milk, stock and oats to the leeks, and simmer gently for 10 minutes to thicken the broth.

When the leeks and oats are cooked and the soup has thickened to your liking, add the chives, cream and seasoning, and serve.

6 SERVINGS

10 MINUTES PREPARATION

30 MINUTES COOKING

800ml milk
800ml chicken stock
Pinch ground nutmeg
80g pinhead oats
80g butter
4 large leeks, sliced
5g chives, chopped
2 tablespoons single cream
White pepper
Salt

Carrot, Parsnip, Yoghurt and Lemon Thyme

Carrots and parsnips are the stars of this very simple soup. Naturally sweet, they work perfectly with the tarter flavours of the yoghurt and lemon thyme. The yoghurt also gives this soup a wonderfully velvety finish.

Melt the butter in a large saucepan and sweat the onion for 10 minutes.

Add the cumin and cook for a few minutes, then add the carrots, parsnips, lemon thyme and stock. Cover the pan and simmer for 30 minutes.

Add the yoghurt, season and blend the soup. Bring back to temperature, taking care not to boil the soup, as the yoghurt may split.

6 SERVINGS

10 MINUTES PREPARATION

35 MINUTES COOKING

40g butter
1 large onion, chopped
1 teaspoon ground cumin
5 large carrots, chopped
3 large parsnips, chopped
Good pinch lemon thyme, chopped
1.2 litres vegetable stock
65ml natural yoghurt
Salt
Pepper

Irish Fish Chowder

This traditional Irish chowder is simply bursting with fishy flavours. Tender pieces of smoked haddock and salmon are cooked in a rich soup with bacon, potatoes, prawns and plump, juicy mussels. Rich and indulgent, this bowl of chowder makes a comforting and hugely satisfying lunch or supper. Serve with crusty bread spread with Irish salted butter.

Melt the butter in a large saucepan and sweat the onion for 10 minutes. Add the bacon and cook for a further 5 minutes.

Add the potato and the bay to the pan. Stir to loosen any caramelised vegetables sticking to the base of the pan.

Pour in the whiskey and cook for a few minutes, allowing the whiskey to reduce. Add the stock and cook the soup for 10–15 minutes – long enough for the potatoes to start breaking apart.

Stir in the double cream and bring the soup back up to temperature.

Stir the mussels into the soup, then add the rest of the fish and the parsley. Season to taste and stir everything one more time, taking care not to break up the fish.

Cover the pan and simmer gently for 5 minutes. Remove the bay leaf before serving, and any mussels whose shells remain closed.

6 SERVINGS

20 MINUTES PREPARATION

45 MINUTES COOKING

50g Irish salted butter

1 large onion, diced

2–3 rashers smoked streaky bacon, cut into pieces

1 large waxy potato, diced into 2cm cubes

1 bay leaf

25ml Irish whiskey

1.2 litres fish stock

150ml double cream

1kg fresh mussels in their shells

300g salmon, skinned and diced into 2cm pieces

200g smoked haddock, skinned and diced into 2cm pieces

200g prawns or crayfish, shelled and cooked

Good handful flat-leaf parsley, roughly chopped

Salt

Coarse black pepper

Corned Beef Brisket with Cabbage and Potato

The appearance of corned beef in Irish cuisine dates back to the 12th century, when corned beef was described as a rare and valued dish – cattle and salt were both expensive commodities in those days. Here it teams up with traditional Irish favourites, cabbage and potato, to make a hearty feast.

Heat the oil in a large saucepan and sauté the onion, carrots and celery for 10 minutes.

Add the split peas, bay and sage leaves and chicken stock. Cover, and simmer for 40–60 minutes – the yellow peas should be soft but not mushy.

Add the leek, parsley, potatoes, cabbage and beef to the pan. Simmer the soup for 10 minutes, until the leek and the cabbage are cooked.

Season to taste before serving.

6 SERVINGS

10 MINUTES PREPARATION

1 HOUR COOKING

2 tablespoons oil

1 large onion, sliced into
fine half moons

2 medium carrots, cut
into 1cm rounds

2 sticks celery, finely sliced

30g dried yellow split peas

1 bay leaf

1 sage leaf

1 litre chicken stock

1 large leek, finely sliced

5g parsley, chopped

200g new potatoes,
cooked and quartered

200g savoy cabbage or kale,
finely shredded

350g cooked salt beef, shredded

Salt

Black pepper

Colcannon with Ham Hock

The word 'colcannon' comes from the Gaelic *cal ceannann*, which literally means 'white-headed cabbage'. In the past, an Irish maiden would fill her socks with colcannon and hang them on her front door in the belief that the first man through the door would be her future husband! For our recipe, we have substituted kale for the colcannon and recommend serving the dish with Boxty (see page 22).

Parboil both types of potato in a little salted water. Use a separate saucepan for each and set the potatoes aside until needed.

Melt the butter in a large saucepan and sweat the onion, celery and garlic until soft, about 10 minutes.

Add the parboiled floury potatoes, the bay and the stock and cook for 20 minutes. When the potatoes are completely soft, remove the bay and blend the soup until very smooth.

Add the parboiled new potatoes, the kale and the ham hock. Simmer for 5 minutes.

Finally, add the cream, mustard, spring onions and parsley. Season to taste before serving.

6 SERVINGS

15 MINUTES PREPARATION

40 MINUTES COOKING

2 medium floury potatoes, diced into 2cm pieces

200g waxy new potatoes, skin on, cut into pieces

40g butter

1 large onion, finely chopped

1 stick celery, finely chopped

2 cloves garlic, finely chopped

1 bay leaf

1.1 litres chicken or ham stock

50g kale, blanched and chopped

240g pulled ham hock

130ml single cream

1 teaspoon whole-grain mustard

3 spring onions, finely sliced

10g parsley, chopped

Salt

White pepper

Ham Hock with Yellow Split Peas

This traditional recipe has been handed down through the generations and is believed to have originated in the Dingle Peninsula. It is a humble soup with great flavour. Yellow peas split when their thin skins peel off as they dry and the two halves fall apart naturally. The ham hock is traditionally cooked with thyme, shallots and garlic – typical ingredients from the Emerald Isle.

Heat the oil in a large saucepan and sweat the onion, carrots and celery for 10 minutes, until they become transluscent. Add the garlic and cook for 2 minutes.

Add the split peas to the pan, along with the pearl barley, thyme and bay. Pour in the stock and simmer gently for about an hour, or until the peas are soft but still intact. Remove the bay.

Stir in the pulled ham hock and spring onions. Season to taste, bearing in mind that the ham hock will already be fairly salty.

6 SERVINGS

10 MINUTES PREPARATION

1 HOUR COOKING

2 tablespoons oil

1 large onion, chopped

2 medium carrots, cut into 1cm rounds

2 sticks celery, sliced into 1cm pieces

1 clove garlic, crushed

350g dried yellow split peas

100g dried pearl barley

2 sprigs thyme

1 bay leaf

1.3 litres ham or chicken stock

300g pulled ham hock

3 spring onions, finely chopped

Salt

Coarse black pepper

Scotland

To say that food and drink is at the heart of the Scottish way of life would be an understatement; it is its very lifeblood. With rolling, rural highlands, clear coastal waters and fertile ground, Scotland produces some of the best natural produce in the world. From Aberdeen Angus steaks and haggis, to world-renowned trout and salmon, the 'Made in Scotland' stamp has become synonymous with good taste and fine quality.

Haggis, the Scottish national dish, is very special indeed – warm, moist, meaty and spicy, it has to be one of the most comforting foods you'll find. Arbroath smokies originated in Auchmithie, a small fishing village just a few miles north of Arbroath. Only haddock can be used to create this timeless delicacy. The fish is salted then hung in whisky barrels that are dug into the ground to serve as smoke pits. These golden-brown fish are truly mouthwatering.

Scottish soups tend to be thick and hearty, designed to take the chill off a cold winter's evening. Our soups are ingredient-rich and include such favourites as Cock-a-Leekie, Cullen Skink and a Traditional Scotch Broth. We promise that you will enjoy them.

Cullen Skink

Full-flavoured, hearty and comfortingly creamy, cullen skink is one of Scotland's finest fish soups. It is packed with warming wintery ingredients – smoked fish, potatoes and smooth, enriching cream.

Pour the milk into a large saucepan and add the fish and the bay leaf. Bring to the boil and remove from the heat. Allow to cool, then remove the fish from the milk. Discard any skin and bones and flake the fish. Strain and reserve the cooking liquid.

Melt the butter in a large saucepan and sweat the onion and leek, until soft. Do not allow to colour.

Add the potatoes, the fish stock and 660ml of the reserved milk to the pan. Season, and simmer gently for 20 minutes. When the potatoes are soft, remove the pan from the heat. Using a slotted spoon, take out about one-quarter of the leek and potatoes and reserve.

Add the cream and cayenne pepper to the soup and blend until smooth. Stir in the flaked fish and the reserved leek and potatoes. Add the lemon juice and chives and season again if needed.

6 SERVINGS

15 MINUTES PREPARATION

40 MINUTES COOKING

700ml milk

600g smoked haddock

1 bay leaf

60g butter

1 medium onion, chopped

1 large leek, diced

340g floury potatoes,
cut into small pieces

500ml fish stock

60ml single cream

Small pinch cayenne pepper

½ lemon, juiced

Small handful chives, chopped

Salt

White pepper

Burns Night Haggis and Neeps

Based on the traditional Burns Night supper of haggis and turnips (neeps), this recipe is bursting with flavour. We've opted for swedes instead of turnips. Choose small ones for maximum sweetness once combined with the spice of haggis. We suspect this recipe will be one you'll return to year after year.

Heat the oil in a large saucepan and sauté the onion, carrots and garlic for 10 minutes. Add the whisky and cook for a further 5 minutes.

Add the swede, the potatoes, the red lentils and the pearl barley to the pan. Stir, then add the stock and simmer for about 40 minutes, until the lentils have broken down and all the vegetables are cooked and starting to break up.

Add the haggis, the parsley and salt. Bring the soup up to a simmer. The haggis will break down a little, thickening the soup. Add a touch of pepper, if you like, before serving.

6 SERVINGS

15 MINUTES PREPARATION

1 HOUR COOKING

50ml oil

1 large onion, diced

2 large carrots, chopped

1 clove garlic, crushed

25ml Scotch whisky

1 small swede, cut into 2cm pieces

200g waxy potatoes, cut into 2cm pieces

70g dried red lentils

20g dried pearl barley

1.3 litres chicken stock

200g haggis, skin removed and crumbled or roughly chopped

10g parsley, chopped

Salt

Pepper

Traditional Scotch Broth

This brilliant and quintessentially Scottish soup has been a family recipe for many years, handed down through the generations. It still makes a regular appearance at the table for Lesley Loveday's mum. Lesley, our marketing guru, suggests making it with different cuts of meat; it also tastes great with a shin of beef. This broth makes an excellent main-course meal, especially when served with warm, crusty bread.

Place the lamb in a large saucepan, cover with the water and bring to the boil. Add the carrots, onions, leek and turnip to the pan.

A froth might form on the surface of the water – skim this off every so often. Cook for 15 minutes.

Rinse the barley and add it to the pan, together with the parsley, clove, bay leaf, salt and pepper.

Simmer until the barley is soft and the soup has become thick in consistency, about 50 minutes. Stir the soup as it cooks and skim off any fat with a large spoon.

Remove the lamb 15 minutes from the end of cooking and allow it cool a little before stripping the meat from the bones. Discard the bones.

Cut the meat into small pieces and return to the soup. The final broth should be thick enough to stand a spoon up in. Remove the clove and bay before serving.

6 SERVINGS

20 MINUTES PREPARATION

1 HOUR 15 MINUTES COOKING

450g lamb (on the bone
for more flavour)

3 litres cold water

3 large carrots, diced

2 medium onions, diced

1 large leek, finely sliced

1 small turnip or swede, diced

300g pearl barley, soaked overnight

½ bunch fresh curly-leaf
parsley, chopped

1 clove

1 bay leaf

Good pinch salt

Good pinch white pepper

Cock-a-Leekie

As Scotland's national soup, this recipe is not to be missed. A broth of chicken and leeks is thickened with rice and barley to produce a wholesome combination.

Put the chicken thighs, bay and thyme in a large saucepan and cover with the stock. Bring to the boil, then skim the surface, cover, and simmer gently for 1 hour.

Add the carrots and cook for 30 minutes. Using a slotted spoon, transfer the chicken thighs to a plate and allow to cool.

Skim the surface of the stock again and add the rice, the barley and the leeks. Cover, and simmer gently for 30 minutes.

Pick the chicken meat from the bones, discarding the skin and bones. Add the chicken meat to the soup.

Remove the herbs and season the soup with salt and pepper before serving.

6 SERVINGS

10 MINUTES PREPARATION

2 HOURS COOKING

6 chicken thighs, on the bone
2 bay leaves
2 sprigs thyme
1 litre chicken stock
2 large carrots, cut into chunks
35g long-grain rice
35g dried pearl barley
3 large leeks, thinly sliced
Salt
Black pepper

Hot-smoked Salmon with Potato and Peas

This hot-smoked salmon soup is like a hug in a bowl! It has a decadent smoky flavour and is wonderful served with crusty bread. It's the perfect choice for a rainy afternoon.

Melt the butter in a large saucepan and sweat the onion, garlic, leek and celery for 10 minutes.

Add the cauliflower, potato and fish stock, and simmer for 20 minutes, ensuring all the vegetables are soft.

Pour in the milk and blend the soup, adding a little more stock or milk if needed.

Bring to a gentle simmer, then add the peas, spring onions, sliced potatoes, salmon and crème fraiche. Season with salt and white pepper.

Add a squeeze of lemon juice and sprinkle with dill just before serving.

6 SERVINGS

20 MINUTES PREPARATION

40 MINUTES COOKING

40g butter
1 large onion, finely chopped
2 cloves garlic, chopped
1 medium leek, thinly sliced
2 sticks celery, thinly sliced
100g cauliflower, roughly chopped
1 large potato, cut into 2cm pieces
550ml fish stock
430ml milk
85g peas, blanched and refreshed
3 spring onions, finely diced
130g new potatoes, skins on, cooked and sliced
380g hot-smoked salmon
55g crème fraiche
½ lemon, juiced
Salt
White pepper
Small handful dill, chopped, for garnish

Venison Hotch Potch

With deer roaming the Scottish Highlands, is it any wonder that the Scots have so many wonderful recipes for venison? The meat has become increasingly popular in recent years, owing to it being lean and low in cholesterol, yet rich in flavour and with a superb texture. We consider this rich soup to be one of life's true luxuries.

Preheat the oven to 150°C/gas mark 2.

Heat the oil in a large ovenproof saucepan and brown the venison all over. Add the orange peel, rosemary, bay leaf, stock, seasoning, chocolate and juniper berries. Bring to a simmer, cover, and cook in the oven for 1 hour.

Take the soup out of the oven and add the pearl barley, whisky, carrots, onion and turnips. Return to the oven and cook for 40 minutes.

Add the potatoes and return to the oven for a further 20 minutes, or until the potatoes are cooked. Top up the liquid as necessary. The venison should be tender, so cook for longer if necessary.

Finally, add the kale, season, and return to the oven for a further 10 minutes. Remove the bay before serving.

6 SERVINGS

10 MINUTES PREPARATION

2 HOURS COOKING

40ml oil

345g venison haunch, boned and trimmed

2 strips orange peel

1 sprig rosemary, picked and chopped

1 bay leaf

1 litre chicken or beef stock

2 squares dark chocolate

3 juniper berries

60g dried pearl barley

25ml Scotch whisky

2 large carrots, finely chopped

1 large onion, finely chopped

180g turnips or swedes, chopped

180g waxy potatoes, diced

60g kale, roughly chopped

Salt

Black pepper

Creamy Chicken, Wild Mushroom and Tarragon

This very special soup is perfect for any occasion. Some flavours are just natural matches – chicken with tarragon and cream with mushrooms. The four combined are heavenly – the bittersweet tarragon cuts through the cream to add a lovely piquancy to the dish.

Preheat the oven to 180°C/gas mark 4.

Rub the chicken thighs with the oil, place on a roasting tray and roast for 40 minutes. When cool, remove the skin and bones. Shred the chicken meat and reserve.

Melt the butter in a large saucepan and sweat the onion, celery, leek and carrot for 10 minutes. Add the herbs, then the flour and cook for a few minutes more.

Add the chestnut mushrooms, cook a little, then gradually add the chicken stock, making sure that each addition is absorbed into the roux before pouring in the next. Keep a little of the stock back – you may not need it all.

Simmer the soup for 20 minutes, remove the herbs and blend the soup until very smooth.

Drizzle a little oil into a hot frying pan and flash-fry the wild mushrooms. Do not overcrowd the pan and only add seasoning once the mushrooms are cooked. (Salt draws out the moisture and stops the mushrooms colouring nicely.) Add the tarragon and drain the mushrooms from the pan, reserving the liquid.

Add two-thirds of wild mushrooms and their cooking liquid, the cream and the cooked chicken to the soup. Season, and bring back to a simmer. Ladle into bowls and garnish with the remaining wild mushrooms.

6 SERVINGS

30 MINUTES PREPARATION

1½ HOURS COOKING

6 chicken thighs, on the bone
20ml oil, plus extra for drizzling
60g butter
1 medium onion, roughly chopped
1 stick celery, roughly chopped
1 medium leek, roughly chopped
1 small carrot, roughly chopped
1 bay leaf
2 sprigs thyme
2 tablespoons flour
120g chestnut mushrooms, sliced
1.1 litres chicken stock
120g assorted wild mushrooms, chopped
Small handful tarragon leaves, chopped
200ml single cream
Salt
White pepper

Wild Mushroom

This beautifully simple soup creates a real impact. The splash of Madeira wine makes this an elegant starter for a dinner party.

Melt the butter in a large saucepan and sweat the onion for 10 minutes, then add the garlic and sweat for a few more minutes.

Add the dried porcini mushrooms and the Madeira and allow to cook for 1 minute, before adding the chestnut mushrooms. Stir.

Add the herbs and stock and simmer for 20 minutes.

Meanwhile, heat a little oil in a frying pan. Once the oil is hot, fry the mushrooms in batches, making sure they take on a good colour. Drain the mushrooms, add half to the soup and reserve the rest for later.

Remove the bay and thyme, add the seasoning and cream, then blend the soup.

Tip in the remaining wild mushrooms, ladle the soup into bowls and drizzle with truffle oil to finish.

---

6 SERVINGS

30 MINUTES PREPARATION

40 MINUTES COOKING

30g butter

1 large onion, finely chopped

3 garlic cloves, chopped

10g dried porcini mushrooms

100ml Madeira

400g chestnut mushrooms, sliced

1 bay leaf

3 sprigs thyme

1 litre vegetable stock

Oil, for frying

500g assorted wild mushrooms, roughly chopped

125ml single cream

Salt

Black pepper

Truffle oil, for drizzling

Modern British

Traditional British cuisine is enjoying something of a renaissance. This is due, in part, to the rise of organic food growers and small, artisanal producers. Farmers' markets, once little heard of, are now a regular feature in many towns and cities, and offer the perfect opportunity for showcasing the finest local produce. More than ever before, there is an emphasis on home cooking using good recipes and quality ingredients. To reflect these developments in British cuisine, we have taken a collection of classic British soups and added a modern twist of our own – we have 'souped them up'!

Our contemporary soups feature ingredients that have been sourced from around the world – from the superfood quinoa to delicious, salty halloumi cheese. With recipes that include Chunky Roasted Tomato and Carrot, Butternut and Coriander, we have created a perfect fusion of the traditional with the modern.

Carrot, Butternut and Coriander

This is our showcase soup with a twist! It's a lovely, flavoursome, yet healthy, soup that can be made using spring carrots, which are not quite as sweet as summer varieties. The flavour of coriander is thought to be reminiscent of roasted orange peel, which makes the two perfect partners. Serve the soup with plenty of warm, crusty bread.

In a hot, dry frying pan, toast the coriander seeds for 1–2 minutes. You want them to start to pop and toast, but not to burn. Set aside to cool, then crush them using a mortar and pestle.

Melt the butter in a large saucepan and sweat the onion and celery for 10 minutes. Add the garlic, the butternut squash and the carrots.

Pour in the stock, cover the pan and simmer gently for 30 minutes. Blend the soup to your preferred consistency, adding a little more liquid if you like.

Stir in the honey and lemon juice, season, and garnish with a sprinkling of coriander.

6 SERVINGS

20 MINUTES PREPARATION

40 MINUTES COOKING

1 teaspoon coriander seeds
40g butter
1 large onion, chopped
2 sticks celery, chopped
1 clove garlic, chopped
1 large butternut squash, chopped
3 large carrots, chopped
850ml vegetable stock
1 tablespoon honey
½ lemon, juiced
Salt
White pepper
Few leaves coriander, for garnish

Chunky Roasted Tomato

Homemade tomato soup is like the little black dress of soups – everyone needs a recipe for it in their collection. This is ours – chunky and roasted! For that finishing touch, serve the soup with a dollop of mascarpone cheese and pesto.

Preheat the oven to 180°C/gas mark 4.

Spread the onion, celery, plum tomatoes and garlic over a large roasting tray and drizzle with the 50ml of olive oil. Sprinkle with fennel seeds and season with salt and a good few twists of black pepper.

Roast for about 40 minutes – the garlic should be soft and the vegetables softened and lightly coloured. Tip everything into a large saucepan, squeezing the soft garlic from its skins as you do so. Discard the skins.

Add the stock, tomato purée, tinned tomatoes, basil, oregano and balsamic vinegar, and simmer for about 10 minutes.

Blend the soup to your preferred consistency. Season again and add a drizzle of olive oil.

6 SERVINGS

15 MINUTES PREPARATION

40 MINUTES COOKING

1 large onion, roughly chopped
2 sticks celery, roughly chopped
2kg ripe plum tomatoes, halved
8 cloves garlic, skins on
50ml olive oil, plus extra for drizzling
1 teaspoon fennel seeds
500ml vegetable stock
400g tomato purée
400g tinned chopped tomatoes
Good handful basil leaves
Good pinch oregano
Dash balsamic vinegar
Sea salt
Coarse black pepper

Broccoli, Macaroni and Cheese

There's something wonderfully comforting about macaroni and cheese, especially in winter, when you are looking for excuses not to venture outside into the cold. Our soup is rich and cheesy, but with a broccoli twist. This vibrant green member of the cabbage family has two great loves – Cheddar and pepper – both of which feature plentifully in this dish.

Melt the butter in a large saucepan and sweat the onion and celery for 10 minutes. Add the garlic and sweat for a further 2 minutes.

Add the cauliflower, potato, bay leaf and stock to the pan. Simmer for 20 minutes, or until the potatoes and cauliflower are very soft. Remove the bay leaf, add the milk and blend the soup until smooth.

Blanch the broccoli in boiling water for a couple of minutes, then drain and refresh in cold water.

Add the pasta to the soup, along with the broccoli and the Cheddar. Season to taste, and finish off with a pinch of cayenne pepper.

6 SERVINGS

20 MINUTES PREPARATION

30 MINUTES COOKING

50g butter
1 large onion, diced
2 sticks celery, chopped
2 garlic cloves, crushed
1 medium cauliflower, shredded
1 small potato, cut into chunks
1 bay leaf
600ml vegetable stock
200ml milk
1 medium head broccoli, florets finely chopped
320g cooked ditalini pasta or macaroni
200g mature Cheddar, grated
Pinch cayenne pepper
Salt
White pepper

Cucumber and Mint Detox

Pamper yourself with this delicous detoxing, low-calorie soup. Eaten chilled, this vibrant and piquant dish will have you reaching for more. Not only that, but it couldn't be easier to make.

Place all the ingredients in a blender and blitz until perfectly smooth.

6 SERVINGS

10 MINUTES PREPARATION

2 medium ripe avocados, chopped

2 medium apples, chopped

½ medium melon, chopped

2 cucumbers, chopped

100g watercress

Good handful mint

Thumb-sized piece root ginger, chopped

100g natural yoghurt

400ml apple juice

400ml water

½ lime, juiced

Lesley's Sweet Potato and Kale

This delicious combination of deep flavours has been created by our marketing guru Lesley Loveday. A wholesome affair, the soup is power-packed with nutrients – betacarotene from the sweet potatoes and calcium, minerals and fibre from the kale. A splash of chilli sauce gives this satisfying dish a lively kick.

Melt the butter in a large saucepan and sweat the onion until soft. Add the carrots and the sweet potatoes and pour in the stock.

Stir in the sweet chilli sauce, season, and cook the soup for 20 minutes, or until the vegetables are soft.

Add the kale and cook for a further 2 minutes.

Blend the soup until smooth and serve with warm, crusty bread.

6 SERVINGS

10 MINUTES PREPARATION

20 MINUTES COOKING

25g butter
1 large onion, finely chopped
2 medium carrots, finely chopped
2 large sweet potatoes, diced
2 litres vegetable stock
1 tablespoon sweet chilli sauce
100g kale, shredded
Salt
Pepper

Fennel with Beans and Chorizo

This hearty chorizo, white bean and fennel soup warms you right down to your toes and will have your family and friends begging for more. The perfect combination of flavours – sweet fennel, savoury celery, smoked paprika, fragrant fresh herbs and spicy chorizo, makes for a true treat.

Heat 40ml of the olive oil in a large saucepan and sauté the onion, fennel, celery and garlic for 10 minutes, or until soft.

Add the smoked paprika and cook for a few seconds, then add the beans, herbs and stock. Cover, and simmer for 30 minutes. Remove the herbs and blend the soup until smooth.

Heat the remaining oil in a frying pan and fry the chorizo for 3–4 minutes, until cooked and crispy.

Ladle the soup into bowls and spoon a little of the chorizo and the flavoured cooking oil over each one.

6 SERVINGS

15 MINUTES PREPARATION

45 MINUTES COOKING

80ml olive oil
1 large onion, finely chopped
2 medium fennel, finely sliced
1 stick celery, finely sliced
3 cloves garlic, crushed
Pinch smoked paprika
550g tinned cannellini beans, drained
1 bay leaf
2 sprigs thyme
1 litre chicken stock
200g chorizo, finely diced

Nicola's Cauliflower and Halloumi

This cauliflower soup has been created by Nicola Diogenous, head of new-product development, and demonstrates a perfect fusion of culinary cultures. A scrumptious blend of British cauliflower and Greek halloumi cheese is the happy result of Nicola's marriage into a North London Greek Cypriot family.

Melt the butter in a large saucepan and sweat the leeks until soft.

Add the cauliflower, stock, salt and pepper and simmer for 15 minutes, until the cauliflower is soft.

Add the double cream to the pan and blend the soup until smooth.

To make the garnish, heat the oil in a non-stick frying pan and brown the halloumi on all sides. Add the lemon juice and the parsley.

Ladle the soup into bowls and spoon some halloumi onto the surface of each. Drizzle with the cooking oil before serving.

4–6 SERVINGS

15 MINUTES PREPARATION

20 MINUTES COOKING

50g butter
2 medium leeks, sliced
850g cauliflower florets
1.2 litres chicken or vegetable stock
50ml double cream
Salt
Pepper

FOR THE GARNISH

4 tablespoons olive oil
250g halloumi, diced
½ lemon, juiced
2 tablespoons chopped flat-leaf parsley

Nicola's Spiced Chilli Bean

Here's a winning recipe from Nicola Diogenous. As head of one of our development teams, Nicola is accustomed to creating amazing food combinations, and this soup is no exception. A hearty bowl of Mexican-style beans, this is a truly warming dish.

Heat the oil in a large saucepan and sauté the onion and pepper until soft.

Add the garlic, chilli, dry spices, tomato purée and sugar. Season, and cook for 1–2 minutes.

Add the chopped tomatoes, kidney beans and stock. Blend until smooth, adding more water or stock to reach your desired thickness.

Finally, add the coriander and bring the soup back up to temperature. Ladle into bowls and serve with a good spoonful of sour cream.

4–6 SERVINGS

15 MINUTES PREPARATION

20 MINUTES COOKING

3 tablespoons olive oil
2 medium onions, diced
1 medium red pepper, diced
3 cloves garlic, chopped
1 medium red chilli, chopped
2 teaspoons paprika
2 teaspoons ground cumin
2 teaspoons ground coriander
1 tablespoon tomato purée
1 teaspoon sugar
400g tinned chopped tomatoes
400g tinned kidney beans, drained
450ml vegetable or chicken stock
Handful coriander, chopped
Salt
Pepper
60ml sour cream, for serving

Roasted Sweet Potato, Pepper and Coconut

The deep pink of the sweet potato and deep red of the pepper give this soup a delightfully vibrant colour, while the coconut milk adds a tropical flavour.

Preheat the oven to 180°C/gas mark 4.

Roll the sweet potatoes, red onion, peppers and garlic in the oil and spread evenly on a roasting tray. Roast for 40 minutes, until the vegetables are soft and golden around the edges. Squeeze the garlic from its skins and discard the skins.

Put the roasted vegetables into a large saucepan with the vegetable stock and bring to a simmer for 10 minutes. Pour the coconut milk into the pan and blend the soup.

Add lemon juice and chilli to taste, and season the soup before serving.

6 SERVINGS

10 MINUTES PREPARATION

1 HOUR 10 MINUTES COOKING

800g sweet potatoes, chopped

1 medium red onion, chopped

3 medium red peppers, roughly chopped

4 cloves garlic, skins on

40ml olive oil

1.2 litres vegetable stock

300ml coconut milk

½ lemon, juiced

Pinch red chilli flakes

Salt

Pepper

Smoky Pumpkin and Beans

We view this as one of our 'Souper Soups'. Not only does it taste fantastic, but it is super healthy, too. The pumpkin gives the chilli and smoked spices a really great flavour profile, while the medley of beans means the soup is packed full of fibre and complex carbohydrates. A treat without any guilt!

Heat the oil in a large frying pan and sauté the onion, celery and carrot until soft – about 20 minutes with a lid on. Add the garlic towards the end of this time.

Add the spices, bay, Worcestershire sauce and maple syrup. Cook for a short while, then add the passata and the stock. Simmer for 10 minutes.

Add the beans, potatoes, pumpkin, chopped tomatoes, mustard and sage. Cook for 30 minutes, making sure the potatoes and pumpkin are cooked. Remove the bay leaf, season the soup and serve.

6 SERVINGS

15 MINUTES PREPARATION

1 HOUR COOKING

40ml oil

1 large onion, diced

2 sticks celery, diced

1 medium carrot, diced

2 cloves garlic, crushed

½ teaspoon ground cumin

Pinch chilli powder

1 teaspoon smoked paprika

1 bay leaf

1 tablespoon Worcestershire sauce

2 tablespoons maple syrup

400g passata

600ml vegetable stock

200g tinned cannellini beans, drained

200g tinned black-eyed beans, drained

240g tinned kidney beans, drained

200g waxy potatoes, diced

300g pumpkin, cut into chunks

400g tinned chopped tomatoes

1 teaspoon mustard

4 sage leaves, chopped

Salt

Coarse black pepper

Honey-roasted Butternut Squash with Pecorino and Sage

An autumn favourite, butternut squash makes a superb base for a rich, warming soup. Lemon juice, crème fraiche and pecorino cheese transform this recipe from an everyday soup into a creamy, warming bowl of bliss. Pair with a simple side salad and a slice of French bread for a perfect lunch.

Preheat the oven to 180°C/gas mark 4.

Roll the squash and the garlic in the olive oil, honey and paprika, turn onto a large roasting tray and roast for 40 minutes, until the squash is soft and lightly caramelised. Remove from the tray and allow to cool. Squeeze the garlic from its skins and discard the skins.

Melt the butter in a large saucepan and fry the sage leaves for 2 minutes to extract their flavour. Remove from the butter and reserve as garnish.

Add the onion, celery and carrot to the pan and sweat for 10 minutes. Add the cooked squash and the vegetable stock, simmer for 20 minutes, then blend.

Stir in the pecorino, crème fraiche and lemon juice, season, and blend again, adding a little more honey if you like. Season with salt and pepper.

Serve garnished with a drizzle of olive oil, a few pecorino shavings and the fried sage leaves.

---

6 SERVINGS

20 MINUTES PREPARATION

1 HOUR 15 MINUTES COOKING

---

1 large butternut squash, cut into chunks

6 cloves garlic, skins on

50ml olive oil, plus extra for drizzling

1 tablespoon honey, plus extra (optional)

Good pinch smoked paprika

50g butter

Handful sage leaves

1 large onion, finely diced

2 sticks celery, chopped

1 large carrot, chopped

1.2 litres vegetable stock

50g pecorino cheese, grated, plus a few shavings for garnish

2 tablespoons crème fraiche

½ lemon, juiced

Salt

Pepper

Sweetcorn, Sweet Potato and Red Quinoa

This is an easy-to-make, incredibly healthy broth-based soup, filled with sweet potato chunks, fluffy protein-packed quinoa and sweetcorn seasoned with smoked paprika, red chilli and spring onion. We've finished ours with a dash of cream. Top yours with avocado, crushed tortilla chips and more spring onion for true Tex-Mex flare.

Melt the butter in a large saucepan and sweat the onion for 10 minutes, until translucent, then add the garlic and cook for a few minutes longer.

Add half the sweetcorn to the pan, along with the cauliflower and the vegetable stock. Season, and simmer for 10 minutes. Add the milk to the soup and blend.

Add the sweet potatoes to the soup, along with the remaining sweetcorn and the quinoa. Simmer for 20 minutes, or until the sweet potato is cooked.

Add the cream, smoked paprika, spring onions and chilli, then serve.

6 SERVINGS

20 MINUTES PREPARATION

40 MINUTES COOKING

60g butter

1 large onion, chopped

4 cloves garlic, crushed

500g tinned sweetcorn, drained

½ medium cauliflower, roughly chopped

900ml vegetable stock

120ml milk

400g sweet potatoes, diced

15g red quinoa

120ml single cream

Pinch smoked paprika

3 spring onions, sliced

1 medium red chilli, finely chopped

Salt

White pepper

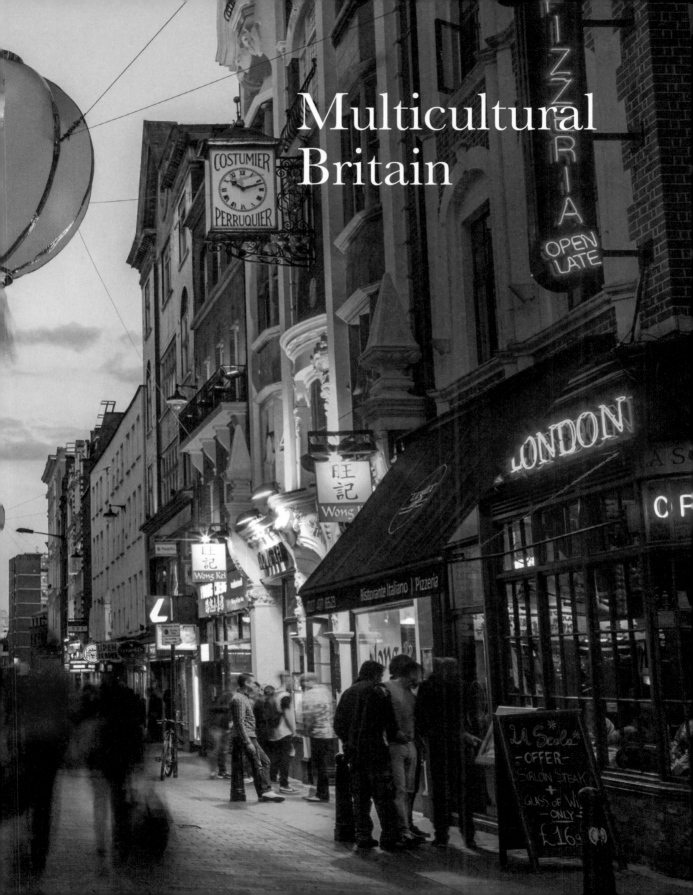

Multicultural Britain

London is the political, economic and cultural capital of Britain. Its history stretches back over thousands of years and, today, it is both a world in one city and a city at the centre of the world. Around 230 languages are spoken within a wealth of different cultures and communities throughout the capital. Britain is now home to over 4.6 million people from other cultures and ethnicities.

British cuisine has long been diverse and multicultural – a mishmash of eclectic styles and flavours that reflect a long history of foreign influences. When the Normans invaded England they brought with them cinnamon, ginger, mace, nutmeg, pepper, saffron and sugar; Victorian explorers introduced exotic ingredients from the far reaches of what was then a vast British Empire.

During the last century, British cuisine has benefitted from the influx of people from varying cultures from all over the globe. Many foods from their diverse cuisines – among them Indian, Chinese, Middle Eastern, Italian and Caribbean – have become assimilated into ours so that ingredients once considered exotic, such as pancetta, cavolo nero, garam masala, tamarind, even garlic and ginger, are now everyday flavourings.

Minestrone Grande with Cavolo Nero

This chunky minestrone soup is based on a traditional Italian recipe that uses butter beans and pasta. Our twist is to add cavolo nero, a great-tasting, nutrient-rich cabbage that gives a real intensity to the flavour of the dish. Finish with a sprinkling of Parmesan cheese or with our Cheesy Croutes (see page 20) for the perfect light supper.

Heat the oil in a large saucepan and sauté the pancetta and the fennel seeds for about 5 minutes, until crispy. Remove, using a slotted spoon, and reserve.

In the same pan, sweat the onion, carrots and celery for 10 minutes, then add the garlic and sweat for another minute.

Add the red and yellow peppers and sweat a little, then add the tomato purée, chilli, paprika, bay, thyme, tomatoes and stock, together with the pancetta and fennel seeds. Cover, and simmer for 30 minutes, or until the vegetables have softened.

Add the pasta and the beans and cook for 10 minutes, until the pasta is nearly cooked. Add the courgettes and cook for a further 5 minutes.

Blanch the cavolo nero and French beans for 5 minutes in boiling water, then add to the soup. Remove the bay and chilli, season, and add the basil leaves.

Serve topped with grated Parmesan.

6 SERVINGS

20 MINUTES PREPARATION

1 HOUR COOKING

2 tablespoons olive oil
100g pancetta, diced
Pinch fennel seeds
1 medium onion, chopped
2 medium carrots, sliced
1 stick celery, sliced
2 cloves garlic, crushed
1 medium red pepper, diced
1 medium yellow pepper, diced
45g tomato purée
½ medium chilli
½ tsp paprika
1 bay leaf
3 sprigs thyme, leaves stripped
400g tinned chopped tomatoes
1.1 litres vegetable stock
80g orzo pasta
220g tinned cannellini or
butter beans, drained
2 medium courgettes, diced
50g cavolo nero, roughly chopped
60g French beans, cut into thirds
Handful basil leaves, torn
Salt
Black pepper
Grated Parmesan, for serving

Mushroom and Spelt

This nutty spelt soup is packed with pancetta, wild mushrooms and fresh herbs. If you would prefer to make this a vegetarian soup, simply leave out the pancetta. Spelt is wonderful in a recipe like this, because it soaks up all the strong flavours.

Heat the oil in a large saucepan and sauté the pancetta until golden. Remove from the oil using a slotted spoon and reserve until later.

Using the same pan, sauté the onion and the celery for 10 minutes. Then add the garlic and, 10 minutes later, the herbs.

Melt the butter in a separate large saucepan, and brown the chestnut mushrooms in batches. When done, add the Madeira and the dried mushrooms to the pan and cook for 1 minute. Add half of the mushroom mix to the onion mix and reserve the other half for later.

Pour the stock into the pan with the onions and mushrooms. Simmer for 10 minutes, then remove the bay and the thyme and blend the soup.

Add in the spelt and half of the pancetta. Cook for 30 minutes, until the spelt is soft. Season to taste.

Finally, add the remaining mushrooms and pancetta to the soup, along with the cream and the herbs. Season again if needed.

6 SERVINGS

10 MINUTES PREPARATION

50 MINUTES COOKING

40ml oil

280g pancetta, diced

1 large onion, finely chopped

2 sticks celery, finely chopped

1 clove garlic, crushed

2 sprigs thyme

1 bay leaf

30g butter

1kg chestnut mushrooms, sliced

25ml Madeira

5g dried porcini pieces

700ml chicken or ham stock
(or vegetable stock if you are
not using pancetta)

110g spelt

50ml single cream

Good handful parsley

Pinch tarragon

Salt

Coarse black pepper

Beef Shin with Barolo and Spelt

A rich and luxurious stew-type soup, this is deceptively simple to make but provides the most delicious of flavours. The robustness of the Italian Barolo wine adds a deep, oak intensity. This dish is perfect for a chilly day beside a roaring fire.

Preheat the oven to 150°C/gas mark 2.

Melt the butter in a large casserole dish or saucepan and brown the beef shin. Don't overcrowd the pan and work in batches if necessary. Remove the beef using a slotted spoon and set aside.

In the same saucepan, brown the onion, celery and carrots for 5 minutes. Add the garlic and cook for 1–2 minutes, then return the beef to the pan.

Pour in the wine and add the tomato purée. Simmer for a few minutes, then add the beef stock, sun-dried tomatoes, herbs and seasoning. Bring to a simmer, cover, and place in the oven for about 3 hours.

Remove from the oven and add the beans, chopped tomatoes and spelt. Give everything a good stir and top up with more stock or water if needed. Cover and return to the oven for another 40 minutes. Check to see that the beef is starting to break apart and that the spelt is nice and soft. Remove the bay and thyme.

Add the lemon zest and juice to taste – you may not need it all. Add the basil and the parsley and check the seasoning. Add more stock or water, if needed, to reach your preferred consistency.

6 SERVINGS

20 MINUTES PREPARATION

3¾ HOURS COOKING

30g butter
400g beef shin, cut into 3cm pieces
1 large onion, diced
2 sticks celery, sliced
2 medium carrots, cut into chunks
2 cloves garlic, crushed
100ml Barolo or other red wine
100g tomato purée
800ml beef stock
35g sun-dried tomatoes, chopped
1 bay leaf
2 sprigs thyme
100g tinned cannellini beans, drained
400g tinned chopped tomatoes
40g spelt
1 lemon, zested and juiced
Good handful basil, chopped
Good handful parsley, chopped
Good pinch salt
Good pinch coarse black pepper

Ribolita

Ribolita is a famous, hearty, Tuscan potage made with bread and vegetables. It is known as Italian peasant food and has been handed down through many generations of Italian families. The ingredients are simmered gently so that the flavours meld together beautifully, and the croutons are almost like dumplings when soaked in the savoury broth.

Heat the oil in a large saucepan and sauté the onion, carrots and celery for 5 minutes. Add the garlic and fennel seeds and sauté for a further 5 minutes.

Add the passata, stock, thyme, bay leaves and chillies. Stir well and bring to a gentle simmer. Cook for 20 minutes.

Add the cannellini beans to the soup, cover, and simmer for 10 minutes. Then add the kale and simmer for a further 10 minutes.

Season well with salt and pepper. Stir in the chopped parsley and serve the soup over croutons (or torn pieces of dry ciabatta bread).

Drizzle with olive oil and top each bowl with a couple of shavings of Parmesan before serving.

2–4 SERVINGS

20 MINUTES PREPARATION

1 HOUR COOKING

1 tablespoon extra-virgin olive oil, plus extra for drizzling

1 small onion, diced

2 small carrots, diced

2 sticks celery, diced

1 clove garlic, crushed

½ teaspoon fennel seeds

160g passata

1 litre vegetable stock

1 teaspoon chopped thyme

Pinch ground bay leaves

Pinch crushed chillies

400g tinned cannellini beans, drained

60g kale, sliced

Handful parsley, chopped

Croutons

Salt

Black pepper

Parmesan shavings, to serve

Italian Wedding Soup

The name 'wedding soup' came about when the phrase *minestra maritata*, which means 'married soup' was mistranslated. The marriage element had nothing to do with happy couples; instead, it referred to the soup's main ingredients – meat and vegetables – and how well matched they are.

Preheat the oven to 180°C/gas mark 4.

Make the meatballs: Combine all the ingredients in a bowl, mix thoroughly, and mould into 3cm diameter balls. Place on a lined baking tray and chill until you're ready to cook them.

To make the soup, melt the butter in a large saucepan and sweat the onion and carrots for 10 minutes. Add the garlic and cook for a further 5 minutes.

Pour in the stock, add the tomatoes and season. Simmer for 20 minutes.

Cook the meatballs in the oven for 10 minutes. When cooked, drain on some kitchen paper.

Add the orzo pasta to the soup and cook for a further 10 minutes.

Finally, add the cavolo nero and meatballs to the soup. Cook for 10 minutes, season, and serve.

6 SERVINGS

40 MINUTES PREPARATION

40 MINUTES COOKING

50g butter
1 large onion, chopped
2 large carrots, chopped
2 cloves garlic, crushed
1 litre chicken stock
400g tinned chopped tomatoes
100g orzo pasta
150g cavolo nero, shredded
Good pinch salt
Good pinch black pepper

FOR THE MEATBALLS

330g minced beef
200g minced pork
100g breadcrumbs
3 cloves garlic, crushed
4 sage leaves, finely chopped
1 egg, beaten
40g grated Parmesan
Pinch paprika

Bigos

Bigos, known as a hunter's stew, is a Polish national dish that pairs traditional meats with cabbage. Cabbage provides a rich source of vitamin C during the winter months, which is when the vegetable is in season. For this reason, bigos has long been a traditional part of a Polish winter diet. This is a hearty soup for the greatest of meat lovers and is the perfect dish to prepare in advance for an evening with friends.

Preheat the oven to 160°C/gas mark 3.

Heat the oil in a large saucepan and brown the pork belly to get a nice colour. Remove the pork from the pan using a slotted spoon, and reserve.

In the same saucepan, sauté the onion for 10 minutes, then add the bacon and the caraway seeds.

Add the apple and the paprika and cook for a few minutes, then add the tomatoes.

Add the sausage, sauerkraut, new potatoes, browned pork belly, seasoning and stock. The stock should cover the ingredients by about 2cm. Cover, and place in the oven for 1½ hours.

Take the soup from the oven, stir in the savoy cabbage and top up the stock if needed. Cover, and return to the oven for 30–40 minutes. Season and serve.

6 SERVINGS

15 MINUTES PREPARATION

3 HOURS COOKING

20ml oil

300g raw pork belly, cut into 2cm pieces

1 large onion, sliced

80g bacon trimmings

1 teaspoon caraway seeds

1 medium apple, grated

1 teaspoon paprika

400g tinned chopped tomatoes

300g cooked smoked Polish sausage, sliced

200g sauerkraut, drained and rinsed

300g new potatoes, halved

1.2 litres chicken stock

200g savoy cabbage, sliced

Salt

Pepper

Marta's Potato and Garlic Soup

Marta Dzygalo is a member of our quality team and has given us a soup that is tasty, healthy and easy to make. The recipe originated in Poland and reminds Marta of happy childhood days spent at her Grandma's house. Well known among working-class Poles, this thick soup oozes garlic and is perfect for a cold day. A truly satisfying meal in a bowl, it is great served with fried bacon or garlic bread.

Heat the oil in a large saucepan and sauté the onions until they become translucent. Add the sugar and stir.

Once the sugar has melted, add the garlic. When you can smell garlic, stir in the potatoes.

Pour in the chicken stock and cook the soup until the potatoes are soft.

Blend the soup, then add the nutmeg, paprika, cream, salt and black pepper to taste.

6 SERVINGS

10 MINUTES PREPARATION

20 MINUTES COOKING

1 tablespoon rapeseed oil

3 large onions, chopped

1 tablespoon sugar

1 clove garlic, chopped

6 large potatoes, cut into cubes

650ml chicken stock

1 teaspoon ground nutmeg

½ teaspoon paprika

1–2 tablespoons double cream

Salt

Black pepper

Terry's Cream of Lemon Soup

Zesty lemon is the hero of this zingy soup. Surprisingly light, this recipe has Greek Cypriot origins and was created by Terry Darbyson, our process technologist. Terry's family emigrated from Cyprus to London in the 1930s.

Melt the butter in a large saucepan and add the vegetables. Cover the pan and sweat for 5–10 minutes, or until the vegetables are beginning to soften.

Thinly pare the lemons using a potato peeler. Blanch the rinds in boiling water for 1 minute, then drain. Squeeze the lemons to give 75–90ml of juice.

Add the lemon rind and juice to the pan with the stock, bay leaves and seasoning. Bring slowly to the boil, cover the pan, and simmer gently for about 40 minutes, or until the vegetables are very soft.

Cool the soup a little and remove the bay leaves. Push the soup through a sieve or purée in a blender. Return to a clean pan, reheat gently, and stir in the cream. Do not allow the soup to boil. Adjust the seasoning.

4–6 SERVINGS

15 MINUTES PREPARATION

50 MINUTES COOKING

25g butter
2 medium onions, thinly sliced
1 small carrot, thinly sliced
1 stick celery, thinly sliced
2 lemons
900ml chicken stock
2 bay leaves
150ml single cream
Salt
Black pepper

Smoky Tomato and Aubergine

This soup combines two Turkish classics – tomato and aubergine – both thought to have been favourites of 17th-century Ottoman sultans. In Turkey, aubergines are known as 'poor man's meat', but they are so delicious in soups that we prefer to call them 'rich man's treats'! Our twist is to add a smoky flavour to the tomatoes that will transport you straight to the Mediterranean. For an added treat, scatter your soup with Toasted Halloumi Squares (see page 18).

Preheat the oven to 180°C/gas mark 4.

Heat 50ml of the olive oil in a large saucepan and sauté the fennel seeds for 1–2 minutes. Add the onion, celery and garlic, and sweat for 10 minutes, before adding the chilli flakes.

Add the tomatoes, vinegar, stock, tomato purée and thyme and simmer for 20 minutes. Take out a few ladlefuls of soup, blend and return to the pan.

Roll the aubergine in the remaining olive oil, and season with smoked paprika, salt and pepper. Spread the aubergine over a non-stick baking tray and roast in the hot oven for 20 minutes, until soft and brown.

Stir the cooked aubergine, fresh oregano and lemon juice into the soup, and season.

6 SERVINGS

20 MINUTES PREPARATION

40 MINUTES COOKING

100ml olive oil

1 teaspoon fennel seeds

1 medium onion, chopped

2 sticks celery, chopped

4 cloves garlic, crushed

Pinch dried chilli flakes

400g tinned chopped tomatoes

2 tablespoons red wine vinegar

1 litre vegetable stock

150g tomato purée

1 teaspoon chopped thyme

500g (about 2 medium) aubergine, cut into 2cm pieces

2 teaspoons smoked paprika

2 good pinches fresh oregano or Greek basil, chopped

½ lemon, juiced

Salt

Coarse black pepper

Spiced Yoghurt, Lentil and Spinach

This wonderful combination of hot and sour can be found from Turkey through the Middle East. When you combine these ingredients they not only taste great, but also help you absorb nutrients more efficiently.

Melt the ghee in a large saucepan and sweat the onion, garlic, ginger and chilli for 10 minutes. Add the spices and cook for 2 minutes.

Add the lentils and stir to mix well with the spices, then pour in the hot stock. Cover, and simmer for about 40 minutes to 1 hour – you want the lentils soft, but intact.

Stir in the spinach, coriander and nigella seeds – the spinach will wilt almost immediately.

Add the yoghurt to the soup, and season. Heat gently, stirring in the yoghurt, then serve.

6 SERVINGS

10 MINUTES PREPARATION

1¼ HOURS COOKING

60g ghee
1 large onion, finely chopped
4 cloves garlic, crushed
Thumb-sized piece root ginger, grated
1 medium red chilli, chopped
2 teaspoons toasted cumin seeds
1 teaspoon ground coriander
1 teaspoon garam masala
Good pinch turmeric
Good pinch ground cardamom
Small pinch ground nutmeg
250g dried green lentils
1.25 litres vegetable stock, heated
300g baby leaf spinach, roughly chopped
15g coriander, roughly chopped
½ teaspoon nigella seeds
200g natural yoghurt
Salt
Pepper

Harira

Harira is a soup traditionally eaten during the holy month of Ramadan, to break the daily fast that begins at dawn and ends at sunset. The soup is also served on special occasions and, specifically, the morning after a wedding, to fill the guests before their journey home. This North African-inspired soup is flavoured with harissa and spices. Serve with houmous on toast and a dollop of natural yoghurt.

Preheat the oven to 180°C/gas mark 4.

Heat the oil in a large saucepan and sauté the carrot, onion and celery for 15 minutes. Add the garlic, chilli and ginger and sweat for a further 5 minutes.

Add the spices and cook for 2 minutes.

Add the vegetable stock, tomato purée, passata, chickpeas, chopped tomatoes and lentils. Simmer for 30 minutes.

Meanwhile, put the diced peppers and aubergine in a bowl, drizzle with a little olive oil and season. Turn out onto a roasting tray and roast in the oven for 15 minutes. Repeat with the courgette, but roast for 10 minutes.

When the lentils are soft, add the roasted vegetables to the soup, along with the lemon zest and juice. Stir in the coriander and season to taste.

6 SERVINGS

30 MINUTES PREPARATION

1¼ HOURS COOKING

35ml olive oil, plus extra for drizzling

1 large carrot, chopped

1 medium onion, chopped

1 stick celery, chopped

3 cloves garlic, chopped

½ medium red chilli, diced

Small piece root ginger, chopped

¼ teaspoon ground cinnamon

1 teaspoon ground roasted cumin

½ teaspoon ground roasted coriander

½ teaspoon turmeric

800ml vegetable or chicken stock

2 tablespoons tomato purée

110g passata

110g tinned chickpeas, drained

450g tinned chopped tomatoes

60g dried red lentils

2 medium red peppers, diced

2 medium yellow peppers, diced

1 small aubergine, diced

1 medium courgette, cut into chunks

1 lemon, zested and juiced

Handful coriander, chopped

Salt

Coarse black pepper

Ghanaian Sweet Potato and Peanut

Ghanaian soups are sophisticated and involve a liberal use of exotic ingredients and a wide variety of flavours, spices and textures. Peanuts and sweet potatoes are integral to West African cooking. The nutty, aromatic flavours in this soup complement the beautiful colour and fluffy sweetness of the sweet potatoes. Serve with some crushed peanuts thrown on top for extra crunch.

Tip the seeds into a large, dry saucepan and place over a medium heat for 1–2 minutes – you want them to toast and start to pop, but not to burn.

Add the oil to the pan, quickly followed by the onion and the ginger. Cook for 5 minutes, then add the garlic and the chilli flakes.

Add the sweet potatoes, tomato purée and stock, and simmer for 20 minutes, until the potatoes are cooked.

Stir in the peanut butter, coconut milk and cashew nuts, and blend.

Add the lemon juice and bring back to temperature. Season and serve garnished with coriander leaves and chilli, if desired.

6 SERVINGS

15 MINUTES PREPARATION

40 MINUTES COOKING

1 teaspoon cumin seeds

1 teaspoon coriander seeds

2 tablespoons oil

1 medium onion, chopped

Thumb-sized piece root ginger, finely chopped

3 cloves garlic, chopped

Pinch dried red chilli flakes, plus extra for serving (optional)

550g sweet potatoes, cut into 2cm pieces

70g tomato purée

1.2 litres vegetable stock

120g peanut butter

260ml coconut milk

50g cashew nuts

½ lemon, juiced

Salt

Pepper

Coriander leaves, for serving (optional)

Piri-piri Chicken

Piri-piri sauce is Portuguese in origin and can also be found in dishes from Angola, Namibia, Mozambique and South Africa. *Piri-piri* is Swahili for 'pepper pepper'. Our twist on this great tradition is to create our own marinade for the chicken.

Preheat the oven to 180°C/gas mark 4.

Make the rub for the chicken: blend together all the ingredients, except the lemon juice. Rub enough of the mixture over the chicken thighs to coat them and keep the rest for later.

Roast the chicken in a hot oven for 30 minutes. Allow it to cool, then strip the meat from the bones and discard the bones.

In a large saucepan, heat the oil and sauté the onion and the celery for 10 minutes. Add the peppers, followed by the remaining rub mixture and cook for a further 10 minutes.

Add the vinegar and tomato purée to the pan, cook a little, then add the chopped tomatoes. Simmer for 20 minutes.

Add the shredded chicken and warm through. Stir in the sour cream, the lemon juice from the marinade ingredients and the parsley.

6 SERVINGS

30 MINUTES PREPARATION

1¼ HOURS COOKING

600g chicken thighs, skinned
50ml rapeseed oil
1 large onion, finely diced
2 sticks celery, finely diced
2 medium yellow peppers, diced
2 medium red peppers, diced
1 tablespoon white wine vinegar
150g tomato purée
340g tinned chopped tomatoes
600ml chicken stock
60g sour cream
Handful fresh parsley, chopped

FOR THE RUB

2 tablespoons olive oil
2 lemons, zested and juiced
6 cloves garlic, chopped
1 teaspoon paprika
1 teaspoon smoked paprika
1 teaspoon caster sugar
1 tablespoon fresh thyme, picked
Good pinch chilli flakes
Good pinch salt
Pinch black pepper

Haleem Chicken

Haleem is a famous Hyderabadi dish, thought originally to have been an Arabic delicacy, served for centuries in the royal palaces of Saudi Arabia. It is a wholesome recipe that combines chicken, dahl and broken wheat – energising and nutritious ingredients. For a filling meal, serve with naan bread and yoghurt.

Heat the ghee in a large saucepan and sauté the onion, garlic, ginger and chilli for 10 minutes, until soft. Add the spices and cook out for 2 minutes.

Add the mung beans, chickpeas, lentils, split peas, stock, chopped tomatoes and tamarind paste. Cover, and simmer very gently for about 1 hour, adding more stock or water as required. Season to taste.

Add the bulgur wheat and the chicken to the soup and cook for a further 10 minutes.

Stir in the coriander and spring onions before serving.

6 SERVINGS

10 MINUTES PREPARATION

1 HOUR 20 MINUTES COOKING

50g ghee
1 medium onion, finely chopped
5 cloves garlic, crushed
Thumb-sized piece root ginger, chopped
1 medium, medium-heat red chilli, finely chopped
1 teaspoon cumin seeds
1 teaspoon ground coriander
½ teaspoon turmeric
½ teaspoon ground cardamom
4 teaspoons paprika
2 teaspoons mustard seeds
Good pinch black pepper
Pinch chilli flakes
80g mung beans
100g tinned chickpeas, drained
80g dried red lentils
100g dried yellow split peas
1.5 litres chicken stock
200g tinned chopped tomatoes
2 teaspoons tamarind paste
25g bulgur wheat
300g cooked chicken, shredded
10g coriander, roughly chopped
4 spring onions, sliced
Salt

Goan Prawn Masala

The beautiful state of Goa has a delicious cuisine. We took our inspiration from traditional Goan ingredients to create a hot, tangy soup. This vibrant dish is guaranteed to fire up your taste buds and looks stunning on the table, too.

Heat the oil in a large saucepan and sauté the onion for 5 minutes. Add the garlic and the ginger and cook for a further 5 minutes.

Stir in the yellow pepper and add the spices. Cook out for 5 minutes.

Add the fish stock, cook for 10 minutes, then blend. Add the coconut milk, lentils, tomatoes and tamarind paste, and simmer for 30 minutes, or until the lentils have cooked.

Roll the prawns in the curry powder.

Heat a little oil in a pan. When good and hot, add the prawns and cook until no longer translucent. Stir in the nigella seeds.

Pour the soup into bowls and top with the yoghurt followed by the prawns and the coriander.

6 SERVINGS

15 MINUTES PREPARATION

40 MINUTES COOKING

50ml oil, plus a little extra

1 large onion, finely chopped

5 cloves garlic, crushed

2 thumb-sized pieces root ginger, finely chopped

1 medium yellow pepper, chopped

1 teaspoon mustard seeds

½ teaspoon chilli flakes

1 teaspoon cumin seeds

1 teaspoon coriander seeds

1 teaspoon paprika

1 teaspoon turmeric

½ teaspoon ground fenugreek

Good pinch black pepper

600ml fish stock

400g tinned coconut milk

120g dried red lentils

150g tinned chopped tomatoes

1 teaspoon tamarind paste

450g raw peeled tiger prawns, cut into thirds

2 teaspoons mild curry powder

Good pinch nigella seeds

50g natural yoghurt

20g coriander, chopped

Black Dahl and Paneer Cheese

A unique combination of urid dahl and paneer turns these everyday Indian ingredients into a gourmet soup delight! Try serving this dish with naan or roti for an authentic North Indian experience. The urid bean is commonly known as the black gram bean, widely available in Asian supermarkets. If you can't find it, you can use any other dried bean.

Heat the butter or oil in a large saucepan and add the onion, garlic, ginger and red chilli. Cook gently for 10 minutes, then add the spices and cook for a further 5 minutes.

Add the tomato purée, tamarind, chopped tomatoes, urid beans and most of the stock. Cover, and simmer for 1 hour, adding more stock as and when you need it.

Just before you are ready to eat the soup, stir in the paneer, spring onions, lemon juice, coriander and salt. Simmer for 5 minutes.

6 SERVINGS

15 MINUTES PREPARATION

1½ HOURS COOKING

40g butter or 40ml oil

1 large onion, finely chopped

3 cloves garlic, chopped

2 thumb-sized pieces root ginger, chopped

1 medium red chilli, chopped

1 tablespoon ground cumin

1 teaspoon turmeric

1 teaspoon ground coriander

½ teaspoon ground cardamom

Pinch ground nutmeg

Pinch ground cinnamon

Good pinch coarse black pepper

2 tablespoons tomato purée

1 tablespoon tamarind paste

400g tinned chopped tomatoes

250g urid beans (soaked in plenty of cold water overnight, washed and drained)

1.8 litres vegetable stock

400g paneer cheese, cut into small pieces

3 spring onions, sliced

½ lemon, juiced

20g coriander, chopped

Salt

Spicy Bengal Gram

Bengal gram, popularly known as chana dahl, is one of the earliest cultivated legumes used in Indian cuisine. It is a protein-rich supplement with a sweet and nutty flavour. Here, we have added an oil infused with Indian spices to create a delicious, warming dahl soup.

Pour the split peas into a large saucepan, and add the garlic, ginger and bay. Cover with the stock and bring to a simmer. Cook the peas for about 40 minutes, until soft. Remove the bay and blend the peas a little – you don't want it too smooth. Cover again and set aside.

Make the spice-infused oil: toast the cumin and coriander seeds for about 30 seconds in a hot, dry frying pan. As soon as they start to pop and smell nice and toasty, tip them onto a plate and reserve.

In the same frying pan, heat the ghee or oil and add the shallots, ginger and chilli. Cook for about 5 minutes, until they start to brown, then add the sesame seeds, all the spices and the curry leaves. Cook gently for 1 minute and set aside.

Warm the dahl through, adding more water or stock if it's looking too thick. Ladle into bowls, and top with the spice-infused oil and chopped coriander.

6 SERVINGS

10 MINUTES PREPARATION

1 HOUR COOKING

400g dried yellow split peas

4 cloves garlic, crushed

Thumb-sized piece root ginger, chopped

1 bay leaf

1 litre vegetable stock

FOR THE SPICE-INFUSED OIL

½ teaspoon crushed cumin seeds

½ teaspoon crushed coriander seeds

100g ghee or oil

4 shallots, finely sliced

Thumb-sized piece root ginger, finely chopped

1 medium, medium-heat red chilli, finely diced

1 teaspoon sesame seeds

Pinch turmeric

½ teaspoon nigella seeds

Pinch curry leaves

20g coriander, roughly chopped

Chicken and Sweetcorn

This soup is based on recipes originating from the southwest of China. A sprinkling of parsley and good pinch of paprika are the finishing touches, both of which complement the chicken beautifully.

Melt the butter in a large saucepan and sweat the onion for 10 minutes, then add the garlic and cook for 1 minute longer.

Add the stock, sweetcorn and potatoes and simmer for 20 minutes, or until the potatoes have started to break up. Add the milk and blend for a few seconds. You don't want the soup to be too smooth.

Add the chicken and simmer for a few more minutes, then add the parsley, paprika and seasoning. Sprinkle with a few chilli flakes if you like it hot!

6 SERVINGS

10 MINUTES PREPARATION

40 MINUTES COOKING

50g butter
1 large onion, finely diced
1 clove garlic, crushed
750ml chicken stock
420g tinned sweetcorn, drained
400g King Edward potatoes, diced
330ml milk
300g cooked chicken, shredded
Good handful parsley, chopped
Good pinch paprika
Salt
Black pepper
Chilli flakes (optional, for serving)

Egg Drop Soup

Egg drop soup, literally egg flower soup (*dàn huā tāng*), is a household staple across China. It is possibly one of the most soothing and comforting dishes ever invented! When you taste the steaming hot broth and savour the first spoonful of silky egg curd, you will instantly be transported to a different place.

Heat the stock, vinegar, salt, ginger and soy sauce in a large saucepan and bring to the boil.

Mix the cornflour with a little water and whisk into the stock. Cook for a few more minutes.

Bring the soup back to the boil and remove from the heat. Whilst whisking the stock in one direction, slowly trickle the beaten egg into the saucepan in a steady, thin stream – it will coagulate into threads.

Finally, add the sesame oil and spring onions to the soup. Season to taste and serve.

6 SERVINGS

5 MINUTES PREPARATION

10 MINUTES COOKING

1.5 litres chicken stock
3 tablespoons rice wine vinegar
1½ teaspoons ground ginger
1½ tablespoons soy sauce
3½ tablespoons cornflour
4 eggs, beaten
1 tablespoon sesame oil
3 spring onions, finely sliced
Salt

Singapore Noodles

Singapore noodles make a scrumptiously wonderful classic dish that makes you feel vibrant and satisfied. We've added our Singapore noodles to a steaming, semi-sweet curried broth. If you like, top the finished dish with coriander and lime wedges for squeezing.

Make the broth: heat the oil in a large saucepan and sauté the carrot, onion, ginger, garlic and chilli for 10 minutes.

Add the spices and cook out a little, then add the vinegar, honey, sesame oil, soy sauce and stock. Simmer for 20 minutes, then blend and keep warm.

Prepare the noodles: first heat the noodles, either by dipping them into a pan of hot water or by giving them a few minutes in the microwave.

Heat the oil in a wok until smoking, then fry the bacon until crispy. Add the remaining noodle ingredients and fry over a high heat, until the vegetables begin to wilt but are still crispy. Stir the vegetables into the warmed noodles and divide between six bowls. Top with the hot broth to serve.

6 SERVINGS

25 MINUTES PREPARATION

40 MINUTES COOKING

2 tablespoons oil

1 medium carrot, chopped

1 medium onion, chopped

2 thumb-sized pieces root ginger, grated

6 cloves garlic, crushed

1 medium red chilli, chopped

2 teaspoons mild curry powder

1 teaspoon ground cumin

1 teaspoon salt

1 teaspoon Chinese five-spice powder

1 tablespoon rice wine vinegar

1 tablespoon honey

10ml sesame oil

3 tablespoons soy sauce

1.2 litres chicken stock

FOR THE NOODLES

300g cooked egg noodles

2 tablespoons oil

300g bacon lardons

2 large carrots, cut into matchsticks

180g baby corn

150g shiitake mushrooms, sliced

1 medium Romano pepper, sliced into rings

400g tinned water chestnuts, drained and sliced

6 spring onions, sliced

On our
Travels

It is now 150 years since cabinetmaker Thomas Cook organised the very first overseas holiday. This has changed our world; Britain would be a very different place today if it weren't for the boom in travel. The British now take over 42 million holidays each year, making our food choices varied. When travelling we experience a wide range of foods, some of which we like and seek out upon returning home. There is now a huge number of international restaurants in Great Britain, and more of us cook those exotic foods that we loved while away. The soups in this chapter showcase local recipes that we have collected and brought home from countries around world. We have used some of the most delicious ingredients that you can find across our globe. *Bon appétit – buon appetito – provecho –* どうぞめしあがれ *– Mahlzeit – smacznego – afiyet olsun*!

Garbure

Garbure is a traditional recipe from the southwest of France. Eaten daily by the Gascon peasantry, recipes differed from one family to the next and changed with the rhythm of the seasons. A hearty soup studded with chopped vegetables and pork, Garbure is so thick you can stand your spoon up in it. It's a meal all in itself and best enjoyed with a glass of a fine Bordeaux.

Melt the goose fat in a large saucepan and sweat the onion, celery and chopped carrots for 15 minutes, then add the garlic.

Pour in the stock and add the paprika. Simmer for 20 minutes. When the vegetables are soft, blend the soup.

Add the bay, thyme, carrot, potatoes, lentils and rice to the pan. Simmer gently for 40 minutes, then add the ham, flageolet and haricot beans and simmer for a further 20 minutes.

In a separate pan, blanch the cabbage and the French beans in boiling water for a couple of minutes, then drain and add to the soup, along with the remaining ingredients. Bring up to temperature, then serve.

6 SERVINGS

20 MINUTES PREPARATION

1 HOUR 20 MINUTES COOKING

50g goose fat

1 large onion, chopped

2 sticks celery, chopped

2 large carrots, chopped, plus
1 large carrot, cut into half moons

3 cloves garlic, peeled

1 litre chicken stock

1 teaspoon smoked paprika

2 bay leaves

3 sprigs thyme

120g waxy new potatoes,
skin on, quartered

35g dried red lentils

35g red rice

220g pulled ham hock

200g tinned flageolet
beans, drained

120g tinned haricot beans, drained

90g savoy cabbage, chopped

120g French beans, cut into thirds

Pinch tarragon

Good handful flat-leaf
parsley, chopped

Salt

Coarse black pepper

Koshari

Koshari is one of the most famous recipes in Egypt where it has been cooked for many generations. It is the ultimate Egyptian street food. The secret to a great-tasting koshari is a good baharat spice mix.

Heat the oil in a large saucepan and sauté the onion and carrot for 10 minutes so that both gain a little colour. Add the ginger, garlic and chilli and cook for 2 more minutes.

Add the baharat spice and cook for 1 minute, then add the tomato purée and the tinned tomatoes. Stir to mix the ingredients well.

Add the lentils, chickpeas, rice and stock. Simmer gently for 30 minutes.

Season the soup and add the vermicelli pasta. Cook for a further 5 minutes, or until the pasta is soft.

Add the herbs and the lemon zest, and warm the soup through before serving.

6 SERVINGS

15 MINUTES PREPARATION

50 MINUTES COOKING

2 tablespoons oil

1 medium onion, finely diced

1 medium carrot, diced

Thumb-sized piece root ginger, chopped

4 cloves garlic, crushed

½ medium red chilli, finely diced

2 teaspoons baharat spice

110g tomato purée

400g tinned chopped tomatoes

30g dried brown lentils

350g tinned chickpeas, drained

30g brown rice

1 litre vegetable stock

40g vermicelli pasta

Good handful coriander, chopped

Half handful parsley, chopped

1 lemon, zested

Salt

Black pepper

Keralan Fish and Butternut

The southwestern Indian state of Kerala is famed for its coastline lined with coconut palms and rich assortment of spices, both of which are celebrated in this soup. Silky smooth and with just the right amount of spice, we have sweetened this recipe to perfection by adding butternut squash.

Toast the seeds and peppercorns in a hot, dry frying pan for 30 seconds, or until the mustard seeds start to pop. Allow to cool, then grind in a spice blender or mortar and pestle.

Heat the oil in a large saucepan, add the onion, garlic, ginger and chilli, and cook for 10 minutes. Stir the toasted spices into the mix.

Add the coconut milk, stock, paprika, tamarind paste and butternut squash. Cover, and simmer for 20 minutes. Once the squash is cooked, use a potato masher to break the butternut down a little, adding a little more liquid if needed.

Bring the soup to a simmer and carefully drop in the fish. Simmer for no more than 5 minutes, add the coriander, and serve.

6 SERVINGS

20 MINUTES PREPARATION

40 MINUTES COOKING

½ teaspoon brown mustard seeds

1 teaspoon coriander seeds

1½ teaspoons cumin seeds

½ teaspoon black peppercorns

2 tablespoons oil or ghee

1 medium onion, chopped

4 cloves garlic, chopped

Thumb-sized piece root ginger, chopped

1 medium red chilli, chopped

500ml coconut milk

750ml fish stock

2 teaspoons paprika

1 teaspoon tamarind paste

250g butternut squash, cut into chunks

750g trimmed monkfish (or other white fish)

15g coriander, chopped

Sri Lankan Chicken

Sri Lankans love soup and eat it regularly, generally at lunchtime. Lentils are an essential ingredient in the Sri Lankan cuisine and feature frequently in soups. In this dish, the lentils soak up the fabulous fusion of herbs and spices.

Heat the oil in a large saucepan and sweat the onions for 20 minutes. Add the ginger and garlic and cook for a further 5 minutes.

Add the spices and seasoning and cook for 5 minutes.

Add the tomato purée, stock, coconut block and red lentils. Simmer for 20 minutes.

Add the chicken to the soup and simmer for 5 minutes.

Finally, add the lime juice, spinach and coriander. Allow the leaves to wilt a little, then serve.

6 SERVINGS

20 MINUTES PREPARATION

55 MINUTES COOKING

40ml oil
1 medium onion, chopped
1 thumb-sized piece root ginger, chopped
2 cloves garlic, chopped
1 teaspoon turmeric
1 teaspoon mild curry powder
1 teaspoon ground cardamom
½ teaspoon ground cinnamon
Small pinch ground cloves
Pinch cayenne pepper
1 teaspoon ground cumin
40g tomato purée
1 litre chicken stock
100g coconut block
170g dried red lentils
300g cooked chicken, shredded
1 lime, juiced
200g baby spinach, chopped
10g coriander, chopped
Salt
Pinch white pepper

Hot-and-Sour Duck Broth

This comforting hot-and-sour Asian-style broth is made with duck, a meat that works perfectly with spices. The success of the recipe comes from combining hot chilli with the acidity from the vinegar, both of which cut into the indulgent duck liquor. Be sure to follow the quantities for this recipe carefully – it is important to get the balance right.

Preheat the oven to 160°C/gas mark 3.

Start with the duck, placing the legs in an ovenproof dish. Combine the remaining duck ingredients, and pour over the legs, ensuring they are covered. Put a lid on the dish and cook in the oven for 2 hours.

Remove the legs from the stock and allow to cool, then remove the skin and bones. Reserve the meat and the strained cooking liquor.

Heat the chicken stock, garlic, ginger, chilli, soy, vinegar, tamarind paste, salt and the duck cooking liquor into a large saucepan and simmer for 5 minutes.

Get a wok hot on the stove and add a little oil. When smoking, add the duck and flash-fry for 3–4 minutes, until brown. Add the vegetables and stir-fry for 1 minute. Add a dash of the broth and divide the duck and vegetables between six bowls. Top the duck with the remaining broth and sprinkle with coriander.

6 SERVINGS

15 MINUTES PREPARATION

2¼ HOURS COOKING

1.2 litres chicken stock

2 cloves garlic, thinly sliced

2 thumb-sized pieces root ginger, finely sliced

1 medium chilli, finely sliced

4 tablespoons soy sauce

1 tablespoon shaoxing vinegar

2 tablespoons tamarind paste

350ml duck cooking liquor (see below)

Oil, for frying

300g cooked duck meat, shredded (see below)

120g shiitake mushrooms, sliced

6 spring onions, sliced

2 large carrots, cut into matchsticks

Good handful coriander, chopped

Salt

FOR THE DUCK

4 duck legs

100ml soy sauce

500ml water

50g dark brown sugar

40g root ginger, chopped

20g garlic, chopped

2 star anise

4 tablespoons cider vinegar

Tamarind Chicken Broth

Our tamarind chicken broth has a distinctive hot-and-sour taste, the hotness coming from the chillies and the sourness from the tamarind paste. These exotic flavours are common across Southeast Asia.

Heat the oil in a large saucepan and sauté the chopped carrot, onion, ginger, garlic and chilli for 10 minutes.

Add the spices and cook for a further 2 minutes, then add the tamarind paste, soy, mirin and stock. Bring the soup to a simmer.

Add the chicken and the remaining vegetables, and simmer gently for 2 minutes, until the vegetables are cooked.

Finally, add the coriander, season, and serve.

6 SERVINGS

15 MINUTES PREPARATION

6 MINUTES COOKING

2 tablespoons oil

1 medium carrot, chopped; 1 large carrot, cut into matchsticks

1 large onion, chopped

2 thumb-sized pieces root ginger, chopped

5 cloves garlic, chopped

1 medium red chilli, finely chopped

½ teaspoon Chinese five-spice powder

1 teaspoon ground Szechuan pepper

2 tablespoons tamarind paste

80ml soy sauce

150ml mirin

1 litre chicken stock

200g cooked chicken, shredded

140g shiitake mushrooms, sliced

200g baby sweetcorn, halved on an angle

Good handful coriander, chopped

Salt

Tom Kha Gai

Tom Kha Gai is a soup made of chicken (*gai*) cooked in coconut milk (*tom*) that has been infused with galangal (*kha*), lemongrass and kaffir lime leaves. Considered to be Thailand's top soup dish, our interpretaion of this wonderful fusion of flavours is a winner.

Put the water, shallots, lemongrass, chillies, lime leaves, garlic, ginger, galangal and coriander in the bowl of a food processor and blend until smooth.

Heat the oil in a large saucepan and cook the blended paste for 10 minutes. Add the soy sauce, sugar and stock, and simmer for 10 minutes.

Add the chicken, fish sauce, shiitake mushrooms, coconut milk, spring onions and bamboo shoots. Simmer for 10 minutes, or until the vegetables are cooked.

Season the soup and add the desired amount of lime juice. Stir the coriander and basil into the soup. To serve, divide the tomatoes between six bowls and pour the soup over the top.

6 SERVINGS

20 MINUTES PREPARATION

30 MINUTES COOKING

50ml water

4 shallots, chopped

3 sticks lemongrass, chopped

2 medium red bird's-eye chillies, chopped

4 lime leaves

4 garlic cloves, chopped

2 thumb-sized pieces root ginger, thinly sliced

1 thumb-sized piece galangal, thinly sliced

10g coriander stalks

1 tablespoon oil

3 tablespoons soy sauce

1 tablespoon palm or brown sugar

1 litre chicken stock

335g cooked chicken, shredded

1 tablespoon fish sauce

125g shiitake mushrooms, sliced

125g coconut milk

5 spring onions, sliced on an angle

100g bamboo shoots, drained

1 lime, juiced

Handful coriander leaves, roughly chopped

10 Thai basil leaves, torn

100g cherry tomatoes, halved

Pinch salt

Turmeric and Coconut Broth

Maximise on the amazing health benefits of turmeric with this simple soup – you need this recipe in your cooking repertoire! Potent, spicy and filled with goodness, it will always leave you wanting more.

Heat the stock in a large saucepan and add the spices, ginger, garlic and soy.

Bring the soup to a simmer and add the coconut milk and the carrots. Simmer for 5 minutes – you want to keep a little bite to the carrot.

Finally, add the spring onions and coriander, and serve.

6 SERVINGS

10 MINUTES PREPARATION

10 MINUTES COOKING

1.2 litres vegetable stock

2 teaspoons ground roast cumin

½ teaspoon turmeric

Good pinch dried chilli flakes

2 thumb-sized pieces root ginger, finely chopped

3 cloves garlic, grated

2 tablespoons soy sauce

700ml coconut milk

3 large carrots, cut into matchsticks

10 spring onions, sliced on an angle

Handful coriander, chopped

Butternut Prawn Laksa

Laksa is a spiced noodle soup, popular in both Chinese and Malaysian cuisine. A good laksa broth has a perfect balance of warm spices, hot chilli peppers, nutty coconut milk, fresh lemongrass and zingy lime juice. We've added tiger prawns and butternut squash to create this delightful fusion.

Using a food processor, blend the onion, garlic, lemongrass, lime leaves, ginger and chilli until very smooth. Heat 3 tablespoons of the oil in a large saucepan, and sauté this blended mix for 5 minutes.

Add the cumin and turmeric to the pan, and cook a little before adding the butternut squash, palm sugar and stock. Cook for 20 minutes, until the squash is soft.

Pour in the coconut milk and the fish sauce, and blend the soup. Add the lime juice.

Heat the remaining oil in a wok. When just smoking, throw in the corn and the peppers. Cook for a few minutes, then add the prawns. Give everything a good stir and add a ladle of soup to get it all cooking. Add half the spring onions, the basil leaves, and half the coriander leaves to the wok.

Cook the rice noodles, as per their instructions, drain, and divide between six bowls. Place the prawns and vegetables on top of the noodles and ladle the soup over the top. Garnish with the remaining spring onions and coriander.

---

6 SERVINGS

20 MINUTES PREPARATION

30 MINUTES COOKING

---

1 medium onion, chopped

4 cloves garlic

3 sticks lemongrass, finely chopped

3 lime leaves

40g root ginger, chopped

1 medium, hot red chilli

4 tablespoons oil

2 teaspoons ground cumin

2 teaspoons turmeric

400g butternut squash, chopped

25g palm sugar

800ml chicken or vegetable stock

400ml coconut milk

1 tablespoon fish sauce

10ml lime juice

180g baby corn, halved on the angle

2 medium red peppers, cut into strips

300g tiger prawns

12 spring onions, chopped

Handful basil leaves, torn

20 coriander leaves

300g raw rice noodles

Kabocha Squash with Miso and Kale

This is a fabulous recipe that teams kabocha squash with miso, a paste made from fermented soy. Sometimes referred to as Japanese pumpkin, kabocha squash is extremely sweet, very rich and nutty tasting. This unusual combination is definitely worth a try.

Heat the oil in a large saucepan and sweat the onions, garlic and ginger for 20 minutes, until soft.

Add the squash and sweat for a further 5 minutes.

Pour the miso and water into the pan, and season. Cook for 30 minutes, then blend the soup.

Add the remaining ingredients and cook for a further 10 minutes before serving.

6 SERVINGS

15 MINUTES PREPARATION

1 HOUR 10 MINUTES COOKING

2 tablespoons rapeseed oil

2 medium onions, chopped

1 clove garlic, chopped

3cm piece root ginger, finely chopped

1 large kabocha squash, cut into chunks

3 tablespoons white miso

650ml water

1 lime, juiced

½ medium red chilli, chopped

320ml coconut water

2 large handfuls kale, chopped

140g edamame beans

3 spring onions, chopped

200g cooked black rice

20ml coconut milk

½ teaspoon salt

White pepper

Prawn Ramen

This wonderful ramen recipe shows you how easy it is to bring fresh and zingy Asian flavours into your kitchen. This delicious soup is frequently served as a main course in Japan.

Warm the stock in a large saucepan and add the ginger, the soy and the wakame. Bring to a simmer, then put to one side while you cook the noodles.

Cook the noodles according to the packet instructions. Drain, and keep warm.

Return the broth to a simmer and add the vegetables and the prawns. Cook for a few minutes, but don't allow the broth to boil too rapidly.

When the prawns are cooked, divide the warm noodles between your bowls and top with the broth. Finish with a sprinkling of coriander, a squeeze of lime and a drizzle of sesame oil.

6 SERVINGS

10 MINUTES PREPARATION

20 MINUTES COOKING

1.5 litres vegetable or chicken stock

2 thumb-sized pieces root ginger, cut into matchsticks

4 tablespoons light soy sauce

1 teaspoon crushed wakame seaweed

300g dried egg noodles

180g baby corn, halved

460g pak choi, chopped

2 large carrots, cut into matchsticks

3 spring onions, chopped

400g raw tiger prawns

Good handful coriander, chopped

1 lime, juiced

Sesame oil, for drizzling

Miso, Tofu and Pak Choi

This simple recipe is one that you'll make on weeknights once you realise how superbly delicious it is. The miso perfectly enhances the flavours of the pak choi, edamame, broccoli and seaweed.

Put the stock, mirin, soy, chilli and ginger in a large saucepan and bring to a simmer.

Blanch the broccoli for a couple of minutes in boiling water, then drain and cut into fours.

Add the miso to the saucepan, along with the pak choi, edamame beans, broccoli and dried wakame seaweed. Season, and simmer for a further 2 minutes.

Distribute the tofu cubes among warmed bowls, ladle the soup over the top, and serve.

6 SERVINGS

15 MINUTES PREPARATION

15 MINUTES COOKING

1.4 litres vegetable stock

65ml mirin

2 tablespoons soy sauce

1 medium, medium-heat red chilli, thinly sliced

2 thumb-sized pieces root ginger, cut into matchsticks

150g tenderstem broccoli

80ml white miso

300g pak choi, sliced

180g edamame beans

2 teaspoons dried wakame seaweed

300g tofu, diced into small cubes

Salt

Pork Belly Udon

Impress your friends and family with this sensational udon noodle soup. This warming bowl of the most divine slow-cooked pork belly teamed with fragrant udon noodles has a rich and intense flavour that guarantees a real showstopper of a meal. This recipe benefits from preparing the pork a day ahead of eating.

Preheat the oven to 180°C/gas mark 4.

Place the pork belly in an ovenproof casserole dish. Mix the remaining pork ingredients together and pour over the pork – they only need to come halfway up the meat, but more is fine.

Cover the meat and cook in the oven for 3 hours. Cool for 1 hour, then remove the pork from the cooking liquid. Chill both the pork and its cooking liquid for a few hours or overnight.

When you are ready to use the pork, cut it into strips, then cut the strips into small chunks and lay on a baking tray. Remove any fat from the top of the chilled cooking liquid, and discard.

To prepare the soup, pour the stock into a large saucepan, add the reserved cooking liquor, carrots, baby sweetcorn and ginger, and bring to a simmer.

Cook the noodles in a pan of salted water until they are soft. Drain and keep warm.

Pop the sliced pork belly in a hot oven for 10 minutes, until it is warmed through. When the meat is ready add the pak choi and the spring onions to the soup and cook for 2 more minutes.

To assemble, divide the warm noodles between six bowls, do the same with the broth, then top with the pork belly, a squeeze of lime and the coriander.

6 SERVINGS

20 MINUTES PREPARATION

3 HOURS 25 MINUTES COOKING

1.5 litres chicken stock

500ml reserved cooking liquor (see method)

3 medium carrots, cut into matchsticks

190g baby sweetcorn, cut in half on the angle

2 thumb-sized pieces root ginger, cut into matchsticks

300g udon noodles

4 pak choi, sliced

5 spring onions, sliced thinly on an angle

1 lime, juiced

2 handfuls coriander, chopped

FOR THE PORK

1kg pork belly, skin on

4 cloves garlic, chopped

2 thumb-sized pieces root ginger, sliced

Good pinch chilli flakes

3 tablespoons dark brown sugar

3 tablespoons honey

4 star anise

500ml water

200ml light soy sauce

40ml cider vinegar

2 tablespoons sesame oil

Korean Kimchi

Kimchi is a national Korean dish consisting of peppers, vegetables and cabbage. It is thought that the name originated from the word *shimchae*, which means 'salted vegetables'. The Koreans have a history of making kimchi in order to preserve vegetables for their long harsh winters.

Heat the oil in a large saucepan and sauté the onions for 5 minutes, then add the garlic and ginger.

Add the tomato purée, red bean paste, soy and vinegar. Cook for 1–2 minutes, then add the stock and bring to a simmer.

Add the carrot, Chinese leaf and pepper to the soup and simmer for 10 minutes.

Finally, stir in the spring onions and coriander, season to taste and serve.

6 SERVINGS

10 MINUTES PREPARATION

20 MINUTES COOKING

40ml oil

1 medium onion, sliced

5 cloves garlic, chopped

Thumb-sized piece root ginger, chopped

3 tablespoons tomato purée

2 tablespoons red bean paste

20ml soy sauce

40ml rice vinegar

1 litre vegetable stock

1 medium carrot, cut into matchsticks

500g Chinese leaf, chopped

1 medium red pepper, cut into strips

5 spring onions, sliced

Good handful coriander, chopped

Salt

Pepper

Boston Bean Soup

Boston beans can be traced back as early as the 18th century when Boston was a significant exporter of rum, a spirit distilled from fermented molasses. In colonial New England, baked beans were traditionally cooked on Saturdays and left in brick ovens overnight. Molasses was then added to the beans to create the renowned Boston baked beans that we know today.

Heat the oil in a large saucepan and fry the bacon until crispy. Add the onion, carrot and celery and fry gently for 10 minutes, then add the garlic.

Add the muscovado sugar, maple syrup, Worcestershire sauce, bay, mustard, tomato purée and spices. Cook for 1 minute, then add the tomatoes, beans, potatoes and stock. Season and stir, then cover and simmer for 40 minutes. Season again, if needed, and remove the bay.

Ladle the soup into bowls and top each bowl with a handful of grated Monterey Jack cheese.

6 SERVINGS

25 MINUTES PREPARATION

50 MINUTES COOKING

40ml oil

160g smoked bacon lardons

1 large onion, finely chopped

1 large carrot, finely chopped

1 stick celery, finely chopped

2 cloves garlic, finely chopped

20g muscovado sugar

20ml maple syrup

1 tablespoon Worcestershire sauce

1 bay leaf

20ml Dijon mustard

90g tomato purée

Pinch chilli flakes

3 teaspoons smoked paprika

400g tinned chopped tomatoes

150g tinned haricot beans, drained

100g tinned black-eyed beans, drained

100g tinned kidney beans, drained

220g potatoes, peeled and cut into chunks

700ml chicken or ham stock

100g Monterey Jack cheese, grated

Salt

Pepper

Cajun Crab and Shrimp Gumbo

When the first French settlers arrived in Louisiana, they took with them their love of bouillabaisse. Lacking any typical French ingredients, the dish was soon unrecognisable as bouillabaisse and became known as 'Gumbo'. Today, it is a classic Cajun, one-pot, communal dish that is eaten in vast quantities around Mardi Gras. We've taken this traditional recipe and added our own twist of crab and prawns.

Heat the oil in a large saucepan and sauté the onion, celery and green pepper for 10 minutes. Add the garlic and the sliced sausage and cook for 5 minutes before stirring in the flour.

Stir in the spices and herbs, then the tomato purée. Cook for 1 minute then add the stock and the tinned tomatoes. Simmer for 10 minutes.

Add the rice and cook for 10–15 minutes, until the rice is cooked.

Add the crab, prawns and spring onions, and season. Simmer for 2 minutes or until the prawns are cooked.

6 SERVINGS

25 MINUTES PREPARATION

45 MINUTES COOKING

20ml oil

1 large onion, finely chopped

2 sticks celery, finely sliced

1 medium green pepper, chopped

3 cloves garlic, crushed

200g andouille or chorizo sausage, sliced

2 tablespoons flour

Pinch chilli flakes

2 teaspoons paprika

½ teaspoon dried oregano

2 tablespoons tomato purée

1.2 litres chicken or fish stock

400g tinned chopped tomatoes

80g rice

250g white crab meat

300g large raw prawns

4 spring onions, sliced

Salt

Good pinch black pepper

Helen's Chilli Chocolate Beef

This fantastic Mexican chilli soup, created by Helen Amos, our marketing guru, is a brilliant dish to serve to friends for a casual get-together. Chilli and smoked paprika make a very strong and warming combination, and they also go perfectly with braised beef. She's included chocolate as her special ingredient, which adds a marvellous depth of flavour. For a final flourish, garnish with sour cream, salsa and chopped coriander, or serve with our Pico de Gallo Salsa (see page 21).

Season the flour and use to coat the beef, shaking off any excess. Heat the oil in a casserole dish and brown the meat on all sides. Work in batches so that you don't overcrowd the pan. Remove the meat from the pan, using a slotted spoon, and reserve.

Using the same saucepan, sauté the onion, celery and garlic for 10 minutes. Add the tomato purée, sherry, spices and bay, and cook for a further 2 minutes.

Return the beef to the pan, then add the passata and the stock. Cover, and simmer gently for 1 hour.

Add the pepper, potatoes and chocolate to the soup and simmer for 30 minutes, or until the new potatoes are beginning to break apart and the meat is tender.

6 SERVINGS

20 MINUTES PREPARATION

2 HOURS COOKING

1 tablespoon flour

1kg stewing beef, cut into 3cm chunks

2 tablespoons oil

1 large onion, sliced

2 sticks celery, sliced

3 cloves garlic, thinly sliced

60g tomato purée

25ml sherry

1 teaspoon smoked paprika

Pinch chilli flakes

2 teaspoons ground cumin (optional)

1 teaspoon ground coriander

1 teaspoon ancho chilli powder

3 bay leaves

200g passata

1 litre beef stock

300g new potatoes, diced

1 medium red pepper, diced

10g dark chocolate

Salt

Good pinch coarse black pepper

Mexican Mariscos

During our winter months, Mexico's beautiful coastal waters yield a wealth of fresh delicacies. This is when *pescados y mariscos* (fish and shellfish) are at their finest. Seafood soup is a speciality of Mexico's Veracruz coast and is found all over Mexico.

Heat the oil in a large saucepan and sauté the onions, garlic and chilli for 10 minutes, then add the cumin seeds and stir.

Add the smoked paprika, white wine, tomato purée, tinned tomatoes and stock, then season.

Simmer for 10 minutes, then add the fish, prawns and squid. Simmer for a further 5 minutes without stirring – you don't want to break the fish up.

Finally, add the lemon juice and parsley, and season.

6 SERVINGS

15 MINUTES PREPARATION

25 MINUTES COOKING

3 tablespoons olive oil

1 large onion, chopped

3 cloves garlic, chopped

1 medium red chilli, chopped

½ teaspoon cumin seeds

1 teaspoon smoked paprika

150ml white wine

20g tomato purée

400g tinned chopped tomatoes

1.1 litres fish or shellfish stock

250g firm white fish, such as monkfish

200g raw tiger prawns

150g squid tubes, thinly sliced

1 lemon, juiced

Handful parsley, chopped

Salt

Pepper

Moqueca

This is our take on *moqueca*, a traditional Brazilian recipe for a fish soup that boasts a beautiful and distinctive flavour. Moqueca has been eaten in Brazil for over 300 years and is thought to have come from the state of Bahia, to the north of the country.

Heat the oil in a large saucepan and sauté the onion for 10 minutes, until it loses its colour. Add the yellow pepper, chilli and garlic, and cook for a further 2 minutes.

Add the cumin, tomato purée and stock. Cover the pan, and simmer for 20 minutes. Once all the vegetables are soft, blend the soup.

Add the turtle beans, red pepper, tomatoes and rice. Simmer for 15 minutes, until the peppers and rice are soft, then add the coconut milk.

Bring the soup to just under simmering, add the fish and the prawns, turn off the heat, and leave to cook with the lid on for 5 minutes.

When the fish is opaque, add the lime juice to taste and half of the coriander and spring onions. Ladle the soup into bowls and garnish with the remaining coriander and spring onions, and a few cherry tomato halves.

6 SERVINGS

15 MINUTES PREPARATION

1 HOUR COOKING

2 tablespoons oil

1 medium onion, sliced

1 medium yellow pepper, chopped

1 medium, medium-heat red chilli, finely chopped

3 cloves garlic, crushed

1 teaspoon ground cumin

50g tomato purée

700ml fish stock

200g tinned turtle beans, drained

1 medium red pepper, chopped

300g tinned chopped tomatoes

40g rice

220ml coconut milk

500g skinned cod fillets, cut into chunks

200g raw tiger prawns, halved

½ lime, juiced

Good handful coriander, roughly chopped

4 spring onions, thinly sliced on an angle

12 cherry tomatoes, halved

Vegetarian Feijoada

Black beans, vegetables and comforting spices are the ingredients that typify a South American favourite – Brazilian *feijoada*. We have created a vegetarian version of this hearty soup. It is perfect topped with our recipe for Pico de Gallo Salsa (see page 21).

Heat the oil in a large saucepan and sauté the onion and carrots for 10 minutes. Add the garlic and spices and cook for a further 2 minutes.

Add the peppers to the pan and cook the vegetables for a few minutes longer.

Add the tomato purée, stock, passata, beans and seasoning. Simmer for 40 minutes. Remove a few ladles of soup from the pan, blend, then return to the pan.

Stir in the lime juice and coriander and season to taste.

6 SERVINGS

20 MINUTES PREPARATION

1 HOUR 5 MINUTES COOKING

40ml oil
1 large onion, chopped
2 medium carrots, chopped
4 cloves garlic, minced
2 teaspoons ground cumin
1 teaspoon paprika
Pinch dried red chilli flakes
1 large red pepper, sliced
1 large yellow pepper, sliced
2 tablespoons tomato purée
1 litre vegetable stock
200g passata
400g tinned black beans, drained
1 lime, juiced
Good handful coriander, chopped
Salt
Black pepper

Peruvian Chicken and Quinoa

This is our take on *Pollo a la Brasa*, the delicious spit-roasted chicken popular in many Peruvian restaurants. Featuring the health food quinoa, this soup is nourishing, comforting and the perfect welcome-home dish after a long, exhausting day.

Heat a dry pan and toast the cumin and coriander seeds, taking care not to burn them. Grind the toasted seeds in a pestle and mortar.

Heat the oil in a large saucepan and sauté the onion, carrot, celery, yellow pepper and garlic for a few minutes. Add the spices and cook a little longer.

Add the stock and the yellow tomatoes to the pan, bring to a simmer and cover. After 20 minutes, blend the soup.

Add the sliced new potatoes, turtle beans and quinoa. Continue to simmer the soup until the potatoes are cooked, about 15 minutes. Add the chicken.

Bring the soup to temperature, add the lime juice and coriander, and season.

6 SERVINGS

25 MINUTES PREPARATION

40 MINUTES COOKING

½ teaspoon cumin seeds

½ teaspoon coriander seeds

50ml olive oil

1 large onion, roughly chopped

1 medium carrot, chopped

1 stick celery, sliced

1 medium yellow pepper, chopped

3 cloves garlic, chopped

Good pinch aji limone chilli powder

½ teaspoon turmeric

½ teaspoon paprika

1 litre chicken stock

80g yellow cherry tomatoes, halved

230g waxy new potatoes, skin on, sliced

100g tinned black turtle beans, drained

30g red quinoa

200g cooked chicken, shredded

1 lime, juiced

Handful fresh coriander

Salt

Pepper

Index

apple, lightly-spiced parsnip
and Bramley apple 93
asparagus
asparagus and
samphire 120–1
Evesham asparagus
risotto with Berkswell
cheese 90–1
watercress, asparagus
and crayfish 72–3
aubergine, smoky tomato and
aubergine 252–3

bacon 49, 246–7,
270–1, 304
and maple popcorn 21
leek, chicken and
bacon cawl 164–5
lentil and bacon 34–5
Stiffkey cockles with bacon
and spinach 114–15
beans
Boston bean soup 304
Cumberland sausage
and beans 134
fennel with beans and
chorizo 220–1
Nicola's spiced chilli
bean 224–5
smoky pumpkin and
beans 228
beef 33, 138–9, 160–1, 244–5
beef shin with Barolo
and spelt 240–1
Burton braised beef 86–7
corned beef brisket with
cabbage and potato 180
Helen's chilli chocolate
beef 308–9
beetroot with Yorkshire
rhubarb 154–5
bigos 246–7
bisque, Cromer
crab 110–11
black pudding crumb
with roasted roots
128–9
blending 9
boxty 22
breads 21, 22–5
breadsticks, pancetta-
wrapped 21
broccoli
broccoli, macaroni
and cheese 215

broccoli and Lancashire
cheese 126–7
cauliflower, broccoli and
Yorkshire Wensleydale
with wild garlic 148–9
Brotchan Roy 174–5
broths 138–9, 194–5,
287, 290
Brown Windsor 33
bubble and squeak 36–7
butternut squash
butternut prawn
laksa 292–3
carrot, butternut and
coriander 210–11
honey-roasted butternut
squash with pecorino
and sage 229
Keralan fish and
butternut 280–1
Tudor's East Anglian
spicy roast butternut
squash 102–3

cabbage 36–7, 246–7
corned beef brisket with
cabbage and potato 180
carrot
carrot, butternut and
coriander 210–11
carrot, parsnip, yoghurt
and lemon thyme 176–7
cauliflower
cauliflower, broccoli and
Yorkshire Wensleydale
with wild garlic 148–9
Nicola's cauliflower and
halloumi 222–3
Shropshire Blue cheese,
cauliflower and
pear 88–9
cavolo nero with minestrone
grande 236–7
cawl 163, 164–5
celeriac
creamy celeriac with
Morecambe Bay
shrimps 136–7
pulled Somerset
ham, celeriac and
parsley 62–3
celery, Fenland celery
and Stilton 106–7
Cheddar chilli crisps 20
cheese
black dahl and paneer
cheese 264–5
broccoli, macaroni and
cheese 215

broccoli and Lancashire
cheese 126–7
cauliflower, broccoli and
Yorkshire Wensleydale
with wild garlic 148–9
cheesy croutes 20
Evesham asparagus
risotto with Berkswell
cheese 90–1
Fenland celery and
Stilton 106–7
honey-roasted butternut
squash with pecorino
and sage 229
rarebit croutons 20
Shropshire Blue cheese,
cauliflower and
pear 88–9
Welsh leek and
Caerphilly cheese
166–7
chicken
Albany's roasted chicken
and parsnip 109
chicken noodle 46–7
chicken and
root vegetable 44
chicken stock 12
chicken and
sweetcorn 267
cock-a-leekie 196–7
creamy chicken, wild
mushroom and
tarragon 202–3
haleem chicken 261
leek, chicken and
bacon cawl 164–5
Peruvian chicken and
quinoa 316–17
piri-piri chicken 260
Somerset scrumpy
chicken 64–5
Sri Lankan chicken 282–3
tamarind chicken
broth 287
tom kha gai 288–9
chilli
Cheddar chilli crisps 20
Helen's chilli chocolate
beef 308–9
Nicola's spiced chilli
bean 224–5
chocolate chilli
beef 308–9
chorizo
fennel with beans and
chorizo 220–1
Laura's pea, chorizo
and scallop 58–9

chowder 57, 179
cider and white onion 61
cock-a-leekie 196–7
cockles
creamy cockle 'n' mussel
chowder with sweet
potato 168–9
Stiffkey cockles with bacon
and spinach 114–15
coconut
roasted sweet potato,
pepper and coconut
226–7
turmeric and
coconut broth 290
colcannon with ham
hock 182–3
consommé 78–9
crab
Cajun crab and
shrimp gumbo 306–7
Cromer crab
bisque 110–11
Salcombe crab 66–7
crayfish, watercress and
asparagus 72–3
crisps, Cheddar chilli 20
croutons 20
cucumber and mint
detox 216–17
cullen skink 190–1

dahl, black dahl and
paneer cheese 264–5
detox, cucumber and
mint 216–17
duck broth, hot-and-
sour 284–5
dulse with braised
oxtail broth 160–1

egg drop soup 268–9

feijoada, vegetarian 314–15
fennel with beans and
chorizo 220–1
Festive supper 49
fish 310–11, 313
fish stock 16
Irish fish chowder 179
Keralan fish and
butternut 280–1
Nikki's Cornish fish
chowder 57
flatbreads 23
focaccia 23

garbure 276–7
garlic 10

Marta's potato and
 garlic soup 248–9
garnishes 18
Glen's London Particular 39
gram, spicy Bengal 266
gumbo, Cajun crab and
 shrimp 306–7

haddock 57, 179
 cullen skink 190–1
 smoked haddock
  kedgeree 42–3
haggis and neeps,
 Burns Night haggis 193
halloumi 18
 Nicola's cauliflower
  and halloumi 222–3
ham
 ham stock 13
 pulled Somerset ham,
  celeriac and
  parsley 62–3
ham hock 39, 276–7
 colcannon with ham
  hock 182–3
 ham hock with yellow
  split peas 184–5
harira 256–7
hotch potch, venison 201
hotpot, Lancashire 132–3

Italian wedding soup 244–5

kabocha squash with
 miso and kale 295
kale
 kabocha squash with
  miso and kale 295
 Lesley's sweet potato
  and kale 218–19
kedgeree, smoked
 haddock 42–3
kimchi, Korean 303
koshari 278–9

laksa, butternut prawn
 292–3
lamb 33, 130–3, 194–5
 lamb and vegetable
  cawl 163
Lancashire hotpot 132–3
leek
 leek, chicken and
  bacon cawl 164–5
 leek and potato 30
 Welsh leek and
  Caerphilly cheese 166–7
lemon, Terry's cream of
 lemon soup 251

lentil
 lentil and bacon 34–5
 spiced yoghurt, lentil
  and spinach 255
lettuce, pea and dill 74–5

macaroni, cheese and
 broccoli 215
Manx broth 138–9
mariscos, Mexican 310–11
masala, Goan prawn 262–3
meatballs 244–5
minestrone grande with
 cavolo nero 236–7
mint
 cucumber and mint
  detox 216–17
 minted nettles with
  smashed Jersey
  Royals® 80–1
 pea and mint with
  crème fraiche 94–5
 Shropshire pea, mint
  and spinach 96–7
miso
 kabocha squash with
  miso and kale 295
 miso, tofu and pak
  choi 298–9
monkfish and red
 mullet 54–5
moqueca 313
mulligatawny 40–1
mushroom
 creamy chicken,
  wild mushroom and
  tarragon 202–3
 mushroom and spelt 238
 wild mushroom 205
mussels
 Brancaster mussel
  stew 116–17
 creamy cockle 'n' mussel
  chowder with sweet
  potato 168–9

neeps and haggis,
 Burns Night 193
nettle, minted nettles
 with smashed Jersey
 Royals® 80–1
noodles
 chicken noodle 46–7
 pork belly udon 300–1
 prawn ramen 296–7
 Singapore noodles 270–1

oils 10, 11, 18,
 spice-infused 266

onion 8, 10
 Newcastle Brown
  onion 146–7
 Somerset white onion
  and cider 61
ox cheek, Burton
 braised beef 86–7
oxtail broth with
 dulse 160–1

pak choi, miso and
 tofu 298–9
pancetta
 crispy pancetta 20–1
 pancetta-wrapped
  breadsticks 21
paneer cheese and
 black dahl 264–5
parsnip
 Albany's roasted chicken
  and parsnip 109
 carrot, parsnip, yoghurt
  and lemon thyme 176–7
 lightly-spiced parsnip and
  Bramley apple 93
pasta
 broccoli, macaroni and
  cheese 215
 crispy pasta bows 21
pea
 Laura's pea, chorizo
  and scallop 58–9
 pea and mint with crème
  fraiche 94–5
 Shropshire pea, mint and
  spinach 96–7
 summer lettuce with pea
  and dill 74–5
peanut, Ghanaian sweet
 potato and peanut 258–9
pear, Shropshire Blue cheese
 and cauliflower 88–9
peas
 hot-smoked salmon with
  potato and peas 198–9
 Test Valley smoked trout,
  horseradish and
  peas 76–7
pease pudding with
 Saveloy 144–5
pecorino and sage with
 honey-roasted butternut
 squash 229
pepitas, smoky 21
pepper, roasted sweet potato,
 pepper and
 coconut 226–7
pesto 21
pico de gallo salsa 21

piri-piri chicken 260
popcorn, bacon and
 maple 21
pork belly 246–7
 pork belly udon 300–1
potato
 corned beef brisket
  with cabbage and
  potato 180
 crispy wedges 20
 hot-smoked salmon with
  potato and peas 198–9
 leek and potato 30
 Marta's potato and
  garlic soup 248–9
 minted nettles with
  smashed Jersey
  Royals® 80–1
prawn 310–11, 313
 butternut prawn
  laksa 292–3
 Goan prawn
  masala 262–3
 prawn ramen 296–7
pumpkin
 Louise's Lincolnshire
  pumpkin 104–5
 smoky pumpkin and
  beans 228

quinoa
 Peruvian chicken and
  quinoa 316–17
 sweetcorn, sweet potato
  and red quinoa 230–1

rarebit croutons 20
red mullet and
 monkfish 54–5
rhubarb with
 beetroot 154–5
ribolita 243
risotto, Evesham asparagus
 risotto with Berkswell
 cheese 90–1
roasted roots with black
 pudding crumb 128–9

salmon, hot-smoked
 salmon with potato
 and peas 198–9
salsa, pico de gallo 21
samphire and
 asparagus 120–1
sausage 49, 246–7
 Cumberland sausage
  and beans 134
 pease pudding with
  Saveloy 144–5

scallop, Laura's pea, chorizo
and scallop 58–9
Scotch broth 194–5
Scouse 130–1
shellfish stock 17
shrimp
Cajun crab and shrimp
gumbo 306–7
creamy celeriac with
Morecambe Bay
shrimps 136–7
Singapore noodles 270–1
soda bread, seeded 24–5
spelt
beef shin with Barolo
and spelt 240–1
mushroom and spelt 238
spinach
Shropshire pea, mint
and spinach 96–7
spiced yoghurt, lentil and
spinach 255
Stiffkey cockles with bacon
and spinach 114–15
split pea (green), Louise's 113
split pea (yellow) 144–5, 266

ham hock with yellow
split peas 184–5
stew 116–17
stock 9, 12–17
stottie cakes 24
summer allotment 151
sweet potato
creamy cockle 'n' mussel
chowder with sweet
potato 168–9
Ghanaian sweet
potato and peanut
258–9
Lesley's sweet potato
and kale 218–19
roasted sweet potato,
pepper and
coconut 226–7
sweetcorn, sweet
potato and red
quinoa 230–1
sweetcorn
chicken and
sweetcorn 267
sweetcorn, sweet potato
and red quinoa 230–1

tofu, miso and pak
choi 298–9
tom kha gai 288–9
tomato
chunky roasted
tomato 212–13
Isle of Wight tomato
consommé with
cucumber noodles
78–9
smoky tomato and
aubergine 252–3
trout, Test Valley smoked
trout, horseradish and
peas 76–7
turkey
Festive supper 49
Norfolk turkey 118–19
turmeric and coconut
broth 290

udon, pork belly 300–1

vegetable stock 16
venison hotch potch 201

watercress, asparagus and
crayfish 72–3
wild garlic, cauliflower,
broccoli and Yorkshire
Wensleydale 148–9
winter allotment 151

yoghurt
carrot, parsnip, yoghurt
and lemon thyme 176–7
spiced yoghurt, lentil
and spinach 255

Thanks

This book was written with
a combined team passion for
great-tasting food, home-cooking
and for the diverse and beautiful
country in which we are proud
to live. Thanks are given to
our inspiringly creative chefs
here at New Covent Garden
Soup Co, and in particular to
Victoria Brophy and Glen
Roberts. Glen's desire to create
truly memorable, delicious,
regional recipes has resulted
in this gorgeous book, which
will take pride of place in
many kitchens across the UK.
Thanks also to Helen Amos
and Lesley Loveday who
researched and wrote the
book, and then passionately
project-managed its total
creation. Finally, our thanks
are extended to Simon Daley,
Anna Southgate and the team
at Pan Macmillan who helped
make this book a reality. Enjoy!

Picture credits

Abbreviations: b (bottom); bl (bottom left); br (bottom right); t (top); tl (top left); tr (top right)

The following images supplied by Shutterstock.com: 26–27, 206–07 S.Borisov; 28t Dutourdumonde Photography; 28bl stocker1970; 28br Mark Lorch; 32 Namurt; 37tl Gayvoronskaya Yana; 37tr Stock Creative; **37b ChameleonsEye**; 38 Bikeworldtravel; 42 Nick Hawkes; 45tl Dancing Fish; **45tr Oxana Denezhkina**; 45b Fotokostic; 48 Sean Nel; 50–51 Raymond Llewellyn; 52tl Massimiliano Marino; 52tr Monkey Business Images; 52b ian woolcock; 56 Andrew Roland; **60tl Martien van Gaalen**; 60tr Mike Charles; 60b Darren Woolridge; 68–69 Andrew Fletcher; 70tl David Hughes; 70tr graycat; 70b chrisdorney; 80tl Kiev.Victor; 80tr Evgenya Frolova; 80b SpeedKingz; 82–83 tomfoxall; 84tl DJTaylor; 84tr Matthew Dixon; 84b Tupungato; 92 Richard Williamson; 96t Andrew Roland; 96bl Diana Taliun; **96br Svetlana Foote**; 98–99 Matt Gibson; 100t Helen Hotson; 100tr Ingrid Maasik; 100b Radek Sturgolewski; 104 Peter Turner Photography; 108t istetiana; 108bl Elena Shashkina; 108br Artur Bogacki; **112 Radek Sturgolewski**; **119tl Grigoriy Pil**; 119tr davidelliottphotos; 119b Jerome Whittingham; 122–23 Len Green; 124t Steve Buckley; 124bl Capture Light; 124br Marco Saracco; 131 Paul Reid; **135t Undivided**; 135b Dariusz Gora; 139 tr3gin; **140–41 Steve Meese**; 142tl Darren Turner; 142tr chrisdorneyl; 142b yahiyat; 150tl Jamie Farrant; **150tr Air Images**; 150b stevemart; **153 Steve Allen**; 156–57 matt_train; 158tl Fulcanelli; **158tr Andrew Roland**; 158b Paul Cowan; 162tl ISchmidt; 162tr photolike; 162b robbinsbox; 170–71 Kanuman; 172t rarena; 172bl Nella; 172br FotograFFF; **178 Serg Zastavkin**; 186–87 MagSpace; 188t EcoPrintl; 188bl Petr Podrouzek; **188br Mark Caunt**; 192 unknown1861; 197 John A Cameron; 200t Mark Bridger; 200bl Oksana Shufrych; 200br Volodymyr Plysiuk; 204t Phill Beale; 204b Maxsol; 208l Tom Gowanlock; 208tr Baloncici; 208b pcruciatti; 214tl Ubonwan Poonpracha; 214tr tabak lejla; 214b Alastair Wallace; 219, 232–33 Christian Mueller; 226 Celso Diniz; 234tl godrick; 234tr Chris Mole; 234b mikecphoto; 239tl Mirabelle Pictures; 239tr B and E Dudzinscy; 239b Eugenegg; 242tl mythja; 242tr VICUSCHKA; 242b olmarmar; 249 Malivan_Iuliia; 250 Antonio Gravante; **254tl Natasha Breen**; 254tr Olena Kaminetska; 254b Girish Menon; 272–73 Ditty_about_summer; 274tl Richard Ruddle Photography; 274tr Mirelle; 274b woottigon; 283 Anton Gvozdikov; 286tl Aoey; 286tr vainillaychile; 286b Galyna Andrushko; 291 Gautier Willaume; 294tl Arina P Habich; 294tr Danielle Balderas; 294b Jason Vandehey; 302t Edith Frincu; 302tr David Kay; 302b Guitar photographer; 305 Albert Pego; 312t Alfredo Borba; 312bl Wichudapa; 312br Alim Yakubov.

Images listed in **bold** also appear on the cover. All other images by Ian Garlick.